90 Days of Encouragement
Volume 3

These daily devotions are designed to encourage firefighters and first responders to grow in their faith. When life seems to be spiraling out of control, and you don't know where to turn, take comfort in the timeless Word of God.

by

Members
of
FCFInternational

Scripture taken from the King James Version, New King James Version®. Copyright © 1982 by Thomas Nelson. Used by permission. All rights reserved; from the Holy Bible, NEW INTERNATIONAL VERSION®, NIV® Copyright © 1973, 1978, 1984, 2011 by Biblica, Inc.® Used by permission. All rights reserved worldwide; The Holy Bible, English Standard Version® (ESV®) Copyright © 2001 by Crossway, a publishing ministry of Good News Publishers. All rights reserved. ESV Text Edition: 2011; from the Holy Bible, New Living Translation, copyright ©1996, 2004, 2007, 2013 by Tyndale House Foundation. Used by permission of Tyndale House Publishers, Inc., Carol Stream, Illinois 60188. All rights reserved; from THE MESSAGE. Copyright © by Eugene H. Peterson 1993, 1994, 1995, 1996, 2000, 2001, 2002. Used by permission of Tyndale House Publishers, Inc.; the Holman Christian Standard Bible®, Used by Permission HCSB ©1999,2000,2002,2003,2009 Holman Bible Publishers. Holman Christian Standard Bible®, Holman CSB®, and HCSB® are federally registered trademarks of Holman Bible Publishers; Scripture quotations marked NASB are taken from the New American Standard Bible®, Copyright © 1960, 1962, 1963, 1968, 1971, 1972, 1973, 1975, 1977, 1995 by The Lockman Foundation. Used by permission; and Scripture quotations marked NRSV are taken from the New Revised Standard Version of the Bible, Copyright © 1989, by the Division of Christian Education of the National Council of the Churches of Christ in the United States of America. Used by permission. All rights reserved. Scripture taken from the Common English Bible®, CEB® Copyright © 2010, 2011 by Common English Bible.™ Used by permission. All rights reserved worldwide. The "CEB" and "Common English Bible" trademarks are registered in the United States Patent and Trademark Office by Common English Bible. Use of either trademark requires the permission of Common English Bible. Scripture quotations marked (TLB) are taken from The Living Bible copyright © 1971. Used by permission of Tyndale House Publishers, Inc., Carol Stream, Illinois 60188. All rights reserved. When the TLB is being used exclusively in a project: Scripture quotations are taken from The Living Bible copyright © 1971.

Fellowship of Christian Firefighters International Preface

The fire service can be a difficult place to serve in for Christian first responders. Daily we are bombarded with images and events that test our faith to the very core. Firefighters can take comfort and gain encouragement from the truth contained within the Bible and from others in the fire service who have walked down similar roads.

Christianity is more than a religious system that first responders must keep to please God. Christianity is a relationship with a creator God who loves us and dispatched His Son Jesus Christ to pay the penalty for the bad things we have done in life (John 3:16). Almost every first responder will admit that they have sinned against God (Romans 3:23). Some will even have knowledge in the fact that there is a penalty for those sins (Romans 6:23). For those first responders who confess their sins and believe on the Lord Jesus Christ as their Savior, they will inherit eternal life (Romans 10:9).

Once we have begun our relationship with God, it is important for us to strengthen and grow that relationship. In the fire service, we are used to training to improve our skills and abilities. We watch videos, take on-line classes, and even travel to be proficient in our roles as first responders. If we are willing to go the extra mile in our roles as firefighters, why do some Christian first responders choose not to grow in their faith? The same technology available for training firefighters is available to learning more about Christ.

The Fellowship of Christian Firefighters International is here to encourage firefighters and first responders in their faith. Our desire is to provide resources that not only help you to grow in your faith but help you to thrive in the Department God has called you to.

Meet the Authors

Keith Helms - Keith Helms is a retired firefighter. He was a member of the Charlotte Fire Department for 29 years. He and his wife, Jane, have three grown children and five grandchildren with the sixth on the way as of this writing. Keith believed in Jesus Christ as his savior in January of 1980. Early in his relationship with the Lord, Keith was introduced to the ministry of discipleship. His desire to minister in the fire service continues to be focused on discipling others.

Wayne Detzler - Straight after finishing his ministry training at Wheaton Graduate School Wayne, Margaret, and their infant daughter set off for missionary service. Their first assignment was in Germany, where Wayne learned to preach in the atmosphere of a region-wide awakening. Later their son, Mark, was born in Germany before they left for England. For thirteen years they served churches in England, where Wayne also developed a ministry among British police.

In 1983 Wayne and Margaret returned to the United States, where Wayne combined teaching and pastoral ministries. While living in Meriden, CT Wayne became chaplain of the Meriden Fire Department in 1988. He helped to launch a chapter of FCFI. In 1994 he moved to Charlotte, NC where he became chaplain of the Charlotte Fire Department and an active FCFI member. In 2007 he entered his present assignment as chaplain of the Long Hill Fire Department in Trumbull, CT.

The driving force in Wayne's life is making disciples. He takes Matt. 28:19 as a life ministry. Wherever they live,

Wayne seeks for guys to disciple. Whether teaching at a local university or meeting with firefighters, he is always looking for F-A-T fellows. These are people who are Faithful, Available, and Teachable. When Wayne finds them, he meets with them to lead them deeper into the Christian life.

Andy Starnes - Instructor Andrew J. Starnes is a lifelong student of the fire service who has been involved since 1992 (volunteer), before becoming a career firefighter in 1998. He is married to Sarah Starnes, and they have a 7-year-old daughter where they reside in Shelby NC. They worship at Putnam Baptist Church. He is a website contributor on the topics of thermal imaging, fire behavior, leadership, and behavioral health, and faith-based devotions for Fire House Magazine, FDIC, Firefighter Toolbox, Fire Department Concepts, Carolina Fire Rescue Journal, Fellowship of Christian Firefighters, and 247 Commitment.

Andrew is the founder of www.bringingbackbrotherhood.org, a non-profit organization designed to encourage and to provide guidance for firefighters in the area of behavioral health and counseling. Articles for these sites are read in several countries and receive approximately 100,000 views per month.

Andrew also serves as the Deputy Chief for the Kill the Flashover Project. He has been featured on the Firefighter Training Podcast, moderfirebehavior.com, Fire House Magazine, and has presented his tactical thermal imaging course in 23 states and 2 countries outside of the US.

Jonathan Riffe - Jonathan Riffe has been involved in the fire service since 1996 and is a firefighter with the Annapolis Fire Department and Deputy Chief of the Dunkirk VFD. He is a past Lieutenant with the Washington DC Fire Department and past Chief of the Huntingtown Volunteer Fire Department. He is the author of "Thomas Sweatt: Inside the Mind of D.C.'s Most Notorious Arsonist" and was a contributing author in the book, "Pass It On: The Second Alarm." Jonathan lives in Maryland with his wife Carrie. His passions include fishing, crabbing, and traveling.

John Epps - John Epps is currently 30 years old and married to his Beautiful Wife Kayla Epps. They have a four-year-old boy named John Jr, and a little girl on the way named Charity Grace. John's family are members at Riverview Baptist Church in Danville, VA. He was Saved and Born Again on May 7th, 2013, when he received Christ into his Heart, and then Baptized in June of 2013. John then answered the call from God and surrendered to Preach in December of 2014. He completed the Liberty University Online Bible Institute, receiving his Certificate in May of 2017. John will soon receive his Ordination and is looking forward for opportunities to minister. John also is a Firefighter with the City of Danville in Virginia, where he has been on the Department for almost 7 years helping others in times of need.

Johnathan Williams – Johnathan joined the fire service on Sept. 22, 2014 with large metro department in North Carolina, currently at the rank of Firefighter 2, within the 4th Battalion, on Ladder Co. 29. He and wife, Courtney, have an 11-month-old son, Matthias, and have been married for 4 years.

Johnathan dedicated his life to Christ halfway through his undergrad studies in October 2011. A major thanks to that was due to a men's discipleship program, led by his peers involved with Campus Outreach. Since that day, Johnathan has seen the need for such programs as being essential for effectively bringing about life change such as found within FCFInternational. Programs of Discipleship where peers minister to their own, allow members to effortlessly relate to each other and develop relationships that encourage spiritual growth in their walk with our Lord Jesus Christ.

Currently Johnathan is working on his MDiv. at Liberty University Baptist Theological Seminary. His prayer, through this journey, is that the fruits from this education with direction and assistance of the Holy Spirit, will allow for greater effectiveness in reaching and educating those within, and outside, the fire service for years to come.

Craig Duck – Craig Duck has served in the fire service almost his entire life. After hanging out with his dad in an Upstate, New York fire department Craig became a volunteer firefighter in 1981. Craig went on to become a firefighter in the Washington, DC Fire Department and retired as a lieutenant after 28 years of service. Craig continues to serve his community as a volunteer firefighter in Boydton, Virginia. He and his wife, Holly, have 4 grown children. After receiving Jesus Christ as his Lord and Savior, Craig has worked hard to glorify God in the fire service. Craig currently serves as your President/Missionary.

Ladder Testing – Day 1
By Craig Duck President/Missionary

Read I Peter 4:12-19

Encouragement for the day – *"Beloved, do not be surprised at the fiery trial when it comes upon you to test you, as though something strange were happening to you. But rejoice insofar as you share Christ's sufferings, that you may also rejoice and be glad when his glory is revealed."*

I Peter 4:12-13 ESV

Ladder testing is something that today's firefighters and first responders don't usually think about. Typically, the chief will give the company a call and order them to the training academy for ladder testing. The last time I went to get our ladders tested we arrived at the training academy and the company responsible for the testing took over. They removed our ladders from the apparatus and placed them on some sawhorses. Each piece of the ladder was inspected, and then it was put under a strength test. A simple drill was used to simulate the correct weight, and then a determination was made as to the structural integrity of the ladder. Those ladders that failed were cut up and set aside. Fortunately, all our ladders passed that day.

Christian firefighters and first responders should not think it strange that we must go through trials and testing. We are told in advance that we are not exempt from going through difficult days. We are encouraged to rejoice when we see them coming. Remember, our Lord and Savior went through testing His entire earthly life. His ministry began when He was tempted in the wilderness for 40 days. He went on to meet opposition from religious leaders who sought to kill Him. Then He died a cruel death on the cross to pay the penalty for our sins. While it might be a natural reaction for us to shy away from trials, they are designed to make us stronger in our faith. When we go through times of testing remember to run to God and allow Him to carry you through the storm.

Lord, thank you for always being here for me what a blessing to know you never sleep or get tired.

Encouragement should be a standard operating guideline!!

God's Path to Safety – Day 2

By Keith Helms – FCFInternational Board Member and retired Battalion Fire Chief with the Charlotte Fire Department

"Keep me safe, my God, for in you I take refuge."
Psalm 16:1 NIV

When a firefighter is involved with the interior attack at a structure fire, he should always know the way of escape. He should never wait until he is in trouble to try and discover a path to safety.

The competent firefighter observes a structure prior to entering and while inside he continually strives to be aware of his location and the availability paths of escape.

When a Christian realizes that he is in trouble, that he has strayed from the narrow path of holiness, he should already know the route to spiritual safety. The Bible is full of passages that encourage us to return to God. One example is found in Revelation 2:1-7 which is written to the Church in Ephesus. This passage is one of the letters to the seven churches (chapters 2-3). The Church in Ephesus is commended for their good works (v. 2-3). However, they are rebuked for leaving their first love (v. 4). While scholars debate the meaning of "first love", I believe that it refers to our love for God (the Father, the Son, and the Holy Spirit; Read Matthew 22:37).

The letter then provides a three-step path to safety (v. 5). First, they are to remember when they were passionate about their relationship with the Lord. Remember God and His love for us. Remember God's call to holiness. Second, they are to repent. Turn back to the path of righteousness. Third, they are to return to the works that accompanied their first love. Don't wait until you are in spiritual trouble to discover God's path to safety. Consistently studying and obeying God's word not only keeps you aware of the way of escape, it also helps you to avoid unrighteousness.

For further study, read all the letters to the seven Churches (Rev. 2:1-3:22). Consider the close parallel between the seven Churches and the church today. Also, notice the frequent reference to the call to repent.

Notes:

_____

_____

_____

History Lesson – Day 3

By Wayne Detzler – FCFInternational Board Member and Fire Chaplain (retired)

> *"Inasmuch as many have undertaken to compile a narrative of the things that have been accomplished among us, just as those who from the beginning were eyewitnesses and ministers of the word have delivered them to us, it seemed good to me also, having followed all things closely for some time past, to write an orderly account for you, most excellent Theophilus, that you may have certainty concerning the things you have been taught."*
>
> Luke 1:1-4 ESV

Dr. Luke was a constant companion of the Apostle Paul. He seems to have written both Luke and Acts while with Paul under house arrest in Rome. This is good history and a dramatic demonstration of the truth of the Lord Jesus Christ. Every time I step before a history class, I do so in the full awareness that Jesus is alive. . .and He is here! Don't let the world tell you any different.

Devastating Tank Fires – Day 4
By Craig Duck – President/Missionary

Read I Corinthians 6:12-20

Encouragement for the day – *"Flee from sexual immorality. Every other sin a person commits is outside the body, but the sexually immoral person sins against his own body."*
I Corinthian 6:18 ESV

    The devastating tank farm in Deer Park, Texas is in its third day, and the fire is still raging. Currently, there are eight tanks on fire wreaking havoc on the area. A large plume of dark black smoke can be seen for miles and families in the area have been warned to stay inside. Some residents are even becoming sick because of the toxic chemicals in the smoke. The firefighters have been working feverishly to extinguish the flames. At first, they were taking a defensive, containment strategy. Now they are putting every effort to extinguish the fire. The community will be dealing with the effects of this fire for years to come.

    The Bible talks a lot about lust and sexual immorality. Paul encouraged us to flee from it as fast as we can. The image is that of Joseph running away from Potiphar's wife after she tore his clothes off and told him to lay with her. There is no good that will ever come from inappropriate sexual relations. God designed for one husband to be with one wife. Anything else goes against Biblical truth and will cause the one who erred to wreck his life. I have seen it so many times in the fire service. An innocent talk with someone from the opposite sex will eventually destroy your family. Sexual immorality also includes having premarital sex. The Bible warns us of the devastating effects of such actions. Don't wait until you have ruined your family, flee from sexual sins and keep yourself pure in the site of God.

Lord, thank you for this reminder. May I check my actions today and ensure they square with Biblical truth.

Encouragement is the art of pulling someone out of the pit of despair!!

How Great a Love – Day 5

By Jonathan Williams – Firefighter with a large metro fire department in NC and FCFInternational Member

> *"For by grace you have been saved through faith; and that not of yourselves, it is the gift of God; not as a result of works, so that no one may boast."*
>
> Ephesians 2:8-9, NASB

As Christ-Followers, we have been given a gift beyond comparison, one of such value we could never repay. It is a gift in which we are so undeserving to receive at the outset.

Paul reflects on our past as unbelievers in Eph. 2:1-3, describing how far we were from God, being dead in our transgressions, living for indulging the desires of our sinful nature; he ultimately displays that we deserve nothing but God's just wrath.

The beauty of Eph. 2:8-9 is revealed in verses 4 and 5. Here Paul states that because of God's great love for us He, out of his rich mercy, made us alive with Christ. Furthermore, our salvation does not originate with people and our abilities to make God love us through the works we perform. Salvation is not accomplished by human achievement but is an act of God's goodness, grace, and love.

Consequently, no matter how unloved, alone, or far from God you may feel today, remember that God loves you and has always loved you. Even though you sin each day and fall short of the mark, as does everyone, remember Paul's words, *"for all have sinned and fall short of the glory of God"* (Rom. 3:23, NASB). We all make mistakes, we all sin. We are not perfect, nor will we ever be until we meet Christ face to face in Heaven. That doesn't mean, though, that you are not loved, that you are not wanted, that you are too lost to fulfill the life that He has called us to as Christians.

For Christ said, *"For God so loved the world, that He gave His only begotten Son, that whoever believes in Him shall not perish, but have eternal life."* (John 3:16, NASB)

Notes:

_____

_____

_____

_____

Your Strength – Day 6

By Wayne Detzler – FCFInternational Board Member and Fire Chaplain (retired)

After a good night's sleep, I came across this encouraging passage in my regular Bible reading.

"And [God] He said to me, 'My grace is sufficient for you, for My strength is made perfect in weakness.' Therefore most gladly I will rather boast in my infirmities, that the power of Christ may rest upon me. Therefore I take pleasure in infirmities, in reproaches, in needs, in persecutions, in distresses, for Christ's sake. For when I am weak, then I am strong."

2 Corinthians 12:9-10 NKJV

It never ceases to amaze me. In a regular, chapter by chapter reading through the Bible, very often a pointed message of encouragement arises. O Father, thank You that Your strength is at its best when I am at my weakest. Amen.

Rip and Run – Day 7
By Craig Duck – President/Missionary

Read Genesis 39:6-14

Encouragement for the day – *"and after a while his master's wife took notice of Joseph and said, "Come to bed with me!"*

Genesis 39:7 NIV

    Many firefighters and first responders are familiar with the old "rip and run" system that was used to give valuable information to those who were responding on an emergency. The system was simple and straight forward. Each firehouse would have a printer located somewhere near the apparatus and easily accessible for emergency responders. When the 911 center would dispatch a call, all the pertinent information was sent to the printer. Location of the incident, what the emergency was, and any other valuable information the dispatcher would type into the system. A firefighter would simply tear off the sheet, run to the apparatus, and give it to the officer, hence the name "rip and run."

    Today we get a glimpse at a man who determined to follow God no matter what the circumstances were around Him. Joseph was sold into slavery by his brothers, falsely accused, thrown in prison, and forgotten. In all these negative circumstance Joseph kept a positive attitude toward God and faithfully served Him. On one occasion Potiphar's wife tried to get Joseph to have sex with her. Everyone had left the house one day, giving her the perfect opportunity to get Joseph to go to bed with her. Nobody would notice, and the two of them could have a good time. Joseph would have none of this because he knew this violated God's principle. Even though there wasn't anybody in the house but Joseph and Potiphar's wife, God would know. Sin ruins everything, and we should run as quick as we can away from it. Don't let sin ruin your life. Learn what please God and learn to follow Him no matter what is happening around you.

Lord, help me today to obey the truths contained in the Bible. May everything I say and do be pleasing to you.

Encouraging firefighters and first responders to keep the faith!!

Your eternal significance – Day 8

By Andrew Starnes – Battalion Chief with a large metro department in NC and FCFInternational Member

"Those who loved you and were helped by you will remember you. So, carve your name on hearts and not on marble." - C.H. Spurgeon

Too often, people go through their lives failing to see their value. Their perspective is clouded by pain, circumstances, or a lack of encouragement.

Some people are appreciated more while they are alive but never truly realize their significance & impact they have made in others' lives. It is our job to tell them every day how important they are. Christ died for them. That alone makes them priceless.

The world sees peace as an absence of conflict. In Jesus, we have peace during the storm. This is the hope that is within us. That no matter the difficulty, we should take comfort in knowing that He has "overcome the world"

When God touches your life, don't be afraid to share this wonderful event with everyone. Don't dismiss it! Share It!

We are in fellowship with one another to "mutually encourage one another", "carry each other's burdens", and to "love one another".

"For God did not send His Son to condemn the world but to save it"

John 3:17

Remember

You are priceless to God.

God Knows Everything – Day 9

By Jonathan Riffe – FCFInternational member

Read Psalm 139

God knows everything about our faults and failures and our feelings and frustrations, and he also knows what our tomorrow holds.

"Your eyes saw my unformed body; all the days ordained for me were written in your book before one of them came to be."

Psalm 139:16 NIV

From his perspective, God can see past, present, and future all at once. It's comforting to me that he knows everything that is going to happen in my life. He not only knows about the future, he's also there in the future.

Ponder that the next time you are on watch and you think you have everything under control. You can't hide from God!!

Renewed Vigor – Day 10

By Wayne Detzler – FCFInternational Board Member and Fire Chaplain (retired)

David gave this simple instruction to his son, Solomon:

"Now seek the LORD your God with all your heart and soul."

1 Chronicles 22:19 NLT

It reminds us that the life of faith is always dynamic. Each day we seek the Lord anew. Every day we pursue His will with renewed vigor. As we pass through this time of transition in our life and ministry, I have been prompted to seek the Lord and His strength more than ever before. As the prophet Isaiah put it:

"Seek the LORD while He may be found, Call upon Him while He is near."

Isaiah 55:6 NLT

What are some practical ways you can seek the Lord this week? _____

_____

Anger is Only One Letter Away from Danger – Day 11

By Andrew Starnes – Battalion Chief with a large metro department in NC and FCFInternational Member

"Let go of anger and leave rage behind! Don't get upset—it will only lead to evil."

Psalms 37:8 CEB

As a student of the Bible and the fire service, I have seen effects of anger in both areas. God's righteous anger for mankind's evil is just, whereas our anger is seldom righteous. I have personally struggled with anger more than any other emotion in my own life.

We may feel justified in our moment of anger but our perspective is more like an adrenaline pumped amateur who gets tunnel vision. As we all know, this is when we are in grave danger.

Leaders are held to an even higher standard when it comes to controlling their anger.

As a leader our every action, every word, and behavior are under constant scrutiny. The moment that anger rears its ugly head can be a career defining moment for a leader. Our poor choice of words, and the use of hateful words that belittle others to make our point is the poorest example of leadership and may lead others down a dark path of anger.

We must remember these words:

"You cannot present reason or the Gospel, which is love, if in the process of it all anger is dominating the whole conversation" (Ravi Zacharias). So, let us ask ourselves, will we let anger rule over us?

Do we realize at that moment whoever or whatever that has angered us has control over us?
The leader who is in control of their anger is like a mighty river controlled by a dam.
Rather than let the raging flood waters loose thereby destroying all in its path, the leader takes the rivers of anger and turns it into positive energy and slowly releases the waters at the proper moment.
With God's help, anger can be controlled rather than letting anger control us
Who do we want to control our life? God or our anger?

When we allow others to anger us, we have let them take control of our lives. The choice is ours, let's stay accountable and under God's watchful hand not mans.

Established in 1929 – Day 12

By Craig Duck – President/Missionary

Read Genesis 1:1-10

Encouragement for the day – "*In the beginning God created the heavens and the earth. Now the earth was formless and empty, darkness was over the surface of the deep, and the Spirit of God was hovering over the waters.*"

Genesis 1:1-2 NIV

The department I now serve in was established in 1929. Most departments love to promote when they were established and how long they have been serving. The older the department, the more they love to tell everyone how long they have been around. Several times in my career I have attended ceremonies where the department was celebrating 100 or 150 years of service. Since the very beginning of our country, firefighters have been serving their communities. George Washington, the founder of our country, served in the Alexandria Fire Department. Before fire departments were established in an area, the communities had to endure the destructive power of fire.

Today's Christian firefighters and first responders are being bombarded with crazy theories on how the world began. Many of these ideas go to great lengths to explain how the world got started without the help of God. The Bible disagrees with all these theories. Genesis is very clear that the world was created in six literal days, and it was created out of nothing. As we look at anything created, we must conclude that there was an intelligent designer. This master designer was God. No other explanation is credible. Nothing else even comes close to reality. The other thing that is amazing is that this creator God loves His creation more than we can understand and desires to have a personal relationship them.

Lord, thank you for creating me. You have given me talents so that I might serve you, help me to understand how.

Encouraging firefighters and first responders to keep the faith!!

What's in a Name – Day 13

By Keith Helms – FCFInternational Board Member and retired Battalion Fire Chief with the Charlotte Fire Department

"I am the Lord; that is my name; my glory I give to no other, nor my praise to carved idols."

Isaiah 42:8 ESV

In many fire departments, it is common for firefighters to give their coworkers a nick name. Typically, the name is given after some action or characteristic is observed by the other firefighters. Often, the name sticks for the duration of the firefighter's career. In my career, I worked with Peedab, Big Head, Big Daddy, Daddy O, Pookie, Red, Red Bird, Booger, Cuz, Disco, Cloud, Possum, Way Back, Outlaw, Yak Yak, Twig, Pretzel, Bones, T-Rex, Fig, Chunk, Home Slice, Crash, Wormy, Fonzo, et. al. There are many more, but they would not be appropriate for this article.

The Bible gives us many names for God. These names identify Him by His attributes. Unlike our nicknames which are often comical, the names of God in scripture reveal something about His nature, increasing our desire to worship Him and to know Him. Take the time to study each of the names listed below. While the list below is not exhaustive, it will give you a deeper understanding of the nature of the Lord God. As you go through the scriptures, look for additional names for Him. Search for them…consider them…let them direct your prayers. When Christ was telling His followers how to pray in Matthew 6:9, He began with "Our Father in heaven, Hallowed be your name." Glorify His name(s) in all that you do.

The Self-existent One (Gen. 2:4; Exodus 3:14); The Lord Will Provide (Gen. 22:13-14); The Lord Who Heals (Exodus 15:26); The Lord my banner (Ex. 17:15); The Lord of hosts (1 Samuel 1:3)
The Lord is peace (Judges 6:24); The Lord our righteousness (Jeremiah 23:6); The Lord the sanctifier (Ex. 31:13); The Strong and Faithful One (Gen. 1:1-3); The Most High (Isaiah 14:13-14);
Almighty God (Gen. 17:1-20); Everlasting God (Isaiah 40:28); The Strong One (Gen. 16:13);
Lord (Gen. 15:2)

Notes:

_____

_____

_____

Life on the Edge – Day 14

By Wayne Detzler – FCFInternational Board Member and Fire Chaplain (retired)

"I can do all things through Christ who strengthens me."
Philippians 4:13 NKJV

During Sundays after Easter our sermons will focus on the treasures of Philippians. Many years ago my now sister-in-law, Ruth Ellen Craft, gave me a copy of Guy King's powerful little study, THE JOY WAY. This forged a lifelong bond with Paul's epistle to the Philippians. Now in the face of new challenges and diminished strength, it becomes ever more important. God's strength is enough for every challenge of every day. In describing the Philippians' life on the edge Paul penned these words:

"for it is God who works in you both to will and to do for His good pleasure."
Philippians 2:13 NKJV

Why is it important for Christian firefighters and first responders to fully rely on God? _____

_____

A Way of Escape – Day 15
By Craig Duck – President/Missionary

Read I Corinthians 10:1-13

Encouragement for the day – *"No temptation has overtaken you except what is common to humanity. God is faithful, and He will not allow you to be tempted beyond what you are able, but with the temptation He will also provide a way of escape so that you are able to bear it."*
I Corinthians 10:13 HCSB

On the fireground, there are many different tasks that need to be completed to put the fire out. Some companies will be operating with a handline with the goal of putting out the fire and checking for extension. Others, however, will have to work without the aid of the hoseline. These tasks include search and rescue operations and rooftop ventilation. For those companies, it is always good to have a plan of escape just in case conditions deteriorate and you have to bailout. I have always taught firefighters to know fire behavior, building construction and have situational awareness to make competent decisions.

In life we will have difficulties, Jesus reminded us of that in John 16:33. God has never promised to keep us from falling. When we look to solving life's problems our way, which is so typical for firefighters and first responders, we are sure to get in trouble. God knows what we can bear and will only allow us to go through trials according to what He knows we can handle. God will make a way of escape if we would but fully trust in Him and His power for every situation. This should encourage us to flee from sin and cling to God. We cannot fall from sin if we choose to obey God.

Lord, help me today to fully trust in You and your power.

Encouraging first responders to keep the faith!!

Press On – Day 16

The PD Kirby Story

By Keith Helms – FCFInternational Board Member and retired Battalion Fire Chief with the Charlotte Fire Department

"Not that I have already reached the goal or am already fully mature, but I make every effort to take hold of it because I also have been taken hold of by Christ Jesus. Brothers, I do not consider myself to have taken hold of it. But one thing I do: Forgetting what is behind and reaching forward to what is ahead, I pursue as my goal the prize promised by God's heavenly call in Christ Jesus."

Philippians 3:12-14

I was privileged in my career in the fire service to work with some exceptional fire ground officers. The captains that I supervised in Battalion 4 A shift were among the best that ever served in the Charlotte Fire Department. One notable fire ground officer was P.D. Kirby. He was known for aggressive (and safe), interior firefighting. Even when a house had heavy fire conditions, P.D. would see what would happen if he took a nozzle one step into the structure. As the suppression crew would hit the fire, he would then advance forward, one step at the time. Most often, as his crew moved forward, the fire would be knocked down and the incident controlled. Craig Duck, lieutenant in the Washington, DC FD, tells his firefighters that in most fire situations, either they are moving forward or something bad is about to happen. While I agree that, there are occasions when the wise decision is to back up, P.D. and Craig are right in always trying to move forward. That is the goal…to safely move forward and control the fire.

In the letter to the Philippian church, Paul presented a similar mindset. He encouraged the believers to "press on", to move forward in their walk with Christ. Becoming like Christ, the process of sanctification, requires us to keep our eyes on the goal; it requires us to set aside the past and to keep advancing. On most days, sanctification is a "one step at a time" process. But it is always a step forward. Let the words of Phil. 3:12-14 encourage you today. As Craig Duck would probably say, either you are moving forward for Christ or something bad is about to happen.

Notes:

_____

_____

True Prosperity – Day 17

By Wayne Detzler – FCFInternational Board Member and Fire Chaplain (retired)

"Trust in the Lord instead. Be kind and good to others; then you will live safely here in the land and prosper, feeding in safety."

Psalm 37:3 Living Bible

Notice how faith in the Lord is coupled with doing good for others. It is reflected in the teaching of Jesus:

"Love the Lord your God with all your heart, and with all your soul, and with all your strength, and with all your mind. And you must love your neighbor just as much as you love yourself."

Luke 10:27 Living Bible

Our love for the Lord is always revealed in our love for those around us. It starts with our family and extends to our friends and our community. This is, according to David, true prosperity.

How can we demonstrate true love for others in the fire service? _____

We Need More Line – Day 18
By Craig Duck – President/Missionary

Read Romans 12:3-8

Encouragement for the day – *"For as in one body we have many members, and the members do not all have the same function, so we, though many, are one body in Christ, and individually members one of another."*

Romans 12:4-5 ESV

As we were going into the building with our hose for a reported fire in an apartment building the chief came on the air and announced "sixth-floor apartment." The engine company has a 400' attack line that is located at the rear of the apparatus, as well as a standpipe rack that can be used to extend the line. When stretching a line to the sixth floor of this apartment building, everyone needs to do their job flawlessly to reach the reporting apartment. On this particular call, the engine company came up short, forcing the lineman to shout "we need more hose."

Christian firefighters and first responders are part of another team, which has been referred to as the body of Christ. This team also needs everyone functioning together with a common goal to succeed. God has designed every Christian first responder with unique talents and abilities.

Some can teach well; some are great at evangelizing and others at serving behind the scenes. God wants to use you as part of His team to reach other firefighters and first responders, encouraging them to serve Him. When we go through life not fulfilling our mission for God in the fire service we are hindering the rest of the team. It's like leaving a pile of hose outside the building. I would encourage those who have been sitting on the sidelines lately to discover your God-given talent and get in the game. We need more line!

Lord, thank You for giving me talents and abilities to serve You. Help me today to be faithful in serving You in my department.

Encouragement ... take some leave some!!

Every Secret – Day 19

By Jonathan Riffe – FCFInternational member

Suppose you were to stand on a stage while a film of every secret and selfish second of your life was projected on the screen behind you.

Imagine what Christ felt on the cross.

Jesus personally carried all our sins in his body. Gossipers, embezzlers, liars, addicts, murderers, etc. See Jesus? With hands nailed open, he invited God, "Treat me as you would treat them!"

"My God, my God, why did you abandon me?"
Matthew 27:46

Why did Christ scream those words? So that you'll never have to.

Make a list of things you are not proud of:

Lord, forgive me of the things I have done that go against your word. Give me courage to lead a life that is pleasing to you.

Going to Heaven – Day 20

By John Epps – FCFInternational Member

Isn't it going to be great when we get to Heaven? To dwell in the House of The Lord! We will be in awe of His beauty! What a day, Glorious Day, That Will Be!

The King Is Coming!

"One thing have I desired of the Lord, that will I seek after; that I may dwell in the house of the Lord all the days of my life, to behold the beauty of the Lord, and to enquire in his temple."

Psalms 27:4 KJV

What does it mean to you personally to dwell in the house of the Lord?

Why don't firefighters and first responders typically think about heaven?

Church Fires – Day 21
By Craig Duck – President/Missionary

Read Matthew 18:15-20

Encouragement for the day – *"For where two or three are gathered in my name, there am I among them."*

Matthew 18:20 ESV

Many firefighters and first responders have been watching the events in France. The famous Notre Dame Cathedral caught fire while under renovation and over 400 firefighters have been working hard to contain the blaze. The pictures have been spectacular, and people all over the world have watched the firefighters try to put the fire out. This has not been the only church fire in the news lately. In the South, several fires in smaller churches have destroyed those buildings. Fires in these types of structures can be challenging to firefighters and have proved deadly in some instances. Firefighters and first responders must exercise extreme caution when fighting these fires, and a well-coordinated plan of attack is a must.

While a fire in your church can be devastating, for the believer, it should not be the end of the world. The Bible teaches that God does not dwell in a building. Wherever two or three are gathered, He is there. How exciting to know that when we meet in a coffee house after our shift to study the Bible, God is there. We also learn that those who have trusted in Jesus Christ as Lord and Savior have the Holy Spirit living within them. Wow, God Himself living within us to guide us along our journey. This changes everything. God dwells where believers gather, what a blessing to know that God doesn't leave us to try and figure everything out. He actively cares about you and desires for you to meet regularly with other believers (Hebrews 10:24-25) so that you might grow closer to Him.

Lord thank you for this reminder that you are with us no matter where we go and no matter what happens to us.

Encouraging firefighters and first responder to keep the faith!!

The Primary Search – Day 22

By Andrew Starnes – Battalion Chief with a large metro department in NC and FCFInternational Member

"You will seek me and find me when you seek me with all your heart"

Jeremiah 29:13

As a firefighter, we are often assigned to perform a primary or secondary search on the fire ground. We are familiar with the primary search and its purpose to quickly search an area near the fire in hopes to find anyone who may have become lost/trapped.

On the fire ground, when we are told that there is a child in the A/D corner of the bedroom, firefighters know what to do. We are properly suited up, PPE in place, and we have our hand line to protect us along with our tools to assist in search and rescue.

In the story of the lost sheep, the Good shepherd leaves the 99 sheep to save the one lost sheep. From an outsider's perspective we are often guilty of saying "Why would anyone leave 99 to save one?"

Every human being is loved by God and Christ died so that all may live. If we arrive at a house fire and we are told that three of the four children are accounted for but they cannot find their youngest child, you'd better believe we are going to do everything in our power to locate and save that child. We as firefighters understand the value of human life.

Let us examine how much God values our lives:

"God demonstrated His great love in this: While we were yet sinners, Christ died for us" (Romans 5:8).

Why? Because God loves all of His children and every life is important to Him. Each & every one of us!

As we put on our PPE to search for the lost remember that God clothed himself in human flesh and took on the form of a servant to die for you and for me. *"For the Son of Man came to seek and to save the lost"* (Luke 19:10).

Let us consider every day a divine opportunity to search for the lost. Let us reach out with urgency as we realize the flames, we are fighting are the fires of hell. Jesus has made the save and all He asks is that we go and tell others about His rescue plan. Let us courageously search for the lost as we too once were lost.

Spiritual Refreshing – Day 23

By Keith Helms – International Board Member and retired Battalion Fire Chief with the Charlotte Fire Department

Consider this:

Working at a structure fire is very demanding. This is very true at multi-alarm fires in the heat of the summer. Firefighters can quickly become fatigued and dehydrated. It is critical that the IC has a Rehab division so that the personnel can continue to effectively work at the scene. In Charlotte this is often handled by Medics and the Red Cross. Their responsibility is to monitor the physical condition of the firefighters and to refresh them with fluids (and doughnuts) and a brief rest so that they can reengage in fighting the fire.

We are called to provide spiritual rehab to our fellow believers. It is not uncommon for a believer to experience a time of spiritual fatigue and dehydration. When we see a brother or sister who is in this condition, we should be like Philemon. Paul wrote him a letter expressing his joy that Philemon was refreshing the hearts of the saints. Like Philemon, we can be a source of refreshment when our faith and love are strong (verse 5-6); a faith in Christ and love for Him and love for all of the saints (other believers). The goal of the refreshments is to encourage a brother or sister to draw closer to Christ, to rest in Him, and to reengage in the spiritual battle. Being a refresher is to be an encourager.

"But encourage each other daily, while it is still called today, so that none of you is hardened by sin's deception."
Hebrews 3:13 NIV

Always be aware of your brother's condition; monitor his spiritual condition. Then you will know how and when to refresh. Be a refresher. Be a Philemon.

Notes:

_____

_____

_____

_____

Take Courage – Day 24

By Wayne Detzler – FCFInternational Board Member and Fire Chaplain (retired)

Psalms 31 is written from a position of deep distress, yet in the midst of it David affirms his trust in the Lord.

"But as for me, I trust in You, O LORD; I say, 'You are my God.' My times are in Your hand."

Psalm 31:14-15 NKJV

As he comes to the end of the psalm, David urges the worshipers to take courage: *"Be of good courage, And He shall strengthen your heart, All you who hope in the LORD."* (Psalm 31:24 NKJV) So, here is the secret. Even in the darkest hour, we can draw strength and courage from trusting the Lord. As an old song put it: "God is still on the throne, and He will remember His own."

What are practical ways you can become more courageous and less fearful in your personal life? _____

_____

_____

Gun Shot Wound – Day 25

By Craig Duck – President/Missionary

Read Ezekiel 36:22-29

Encouragement for the day – *"And I will give you a new heart, and a new spirit I will put within you. And I will remove the heart of stone from your flesh and give you a heart of flesh."*

Ezekiel 36:26 ESV

When I was a firefighter in the Washington, DC Fire Department back in the early 1990's, we went to a lot of shootings. There were days when we would go up to 10 different scenes, several of which ended in fatalities. During those busy days on Engine Company 10, we had a new medical director take over and developed some new policies we were required to follow on shootings. The main policy was to work every patient. On one call we went to an alley where two individuals were obviously dead. The one patient had a large hole in the chest where the heart was supposed to be located and an even larger hole in his back. We didn't work the victim, and the EMS supervisor was upset. I will never forget Charlie looking at the captain and replying, "There isn't even a heart to do a heart massage with?"

Every person that has been born on this earth has a problem. We are sinners in need of a Savior. It has been said that we are all born with a hole in our heart and everyone is trying to fill that void with something. This is what drives many firefighters and first responders to use drugs and alcohol, have inappropriate relationships, and accumulate vast amounts of stuff. Ezekiel got this concept and told the Israelites that God was going to do an amazing thing in their life. They weren't following God and He was about to turn their hearts of stone into a new heart that desired real worship with the Almighty. God can still change people today. He alone can forgive our sins and restore our relationship with Him. Give God a chance and cry out to Him. See how He can change your life for good.

Lord, thank you for your great salvation, so rich and so free. May I learn to walk in all your ways in the department you have called me to.

Encouragement should be a standard operating guideline!!

Crew Integrity – Day 26

By Andrew Starnes – Battalion Chief with a large metro department in NC and FCFInternational Member

"Just as body though one, has many parts but all its many parts form one body, so it is with Christ"
I Corinthians 12:12 NIV

Firefighters understand the importance of working together. The efficiency of a fire crew who is "riding short" suffers dramatically with the loss of each member. The most recent NIST manpower study verified this.

In life, as in firefighting, it is a relief to know that someone is there to help you bear the load. It gives one great comfort & confidence when facing insurmountable circumstances to have someone by their side to walk with them through the fire.

God designed us for relationship, and this is reiterated in all aspects of our life. We are not meant to be alone.

He wants us to maintain crew integrity by first having a relationship with God, through Christ, and filled with the Holy Spirit. Go and fulfill your role in God's Incident Action Plan by being a part of the body of Christ.

Psalm 108:3-5   Day 27

By Wayne Detzler – FCFInternational Board Member and Fire Chaplain (retired)

"I will give thanks to you, O LORD, among the peoples; I will sing praises to you among the nations. For your steadfast love is great above the heavens; your faithfulness reaches to the clouds."

Psalm 108:3-4 ESV

Our best witness is thankfulness to the Lord. As we give thanks to Him, we spread the good news that He is alive and active in our world today. During the past week we heard numerous expressions of thanksgiving to the Lord, as firefighters and their families shared the goodness of the Lord. Although they are not immune from trouble, they are committed to praise of the Lord. The psalm includes this hymn of praise: *"Be exalted, O God, above the heavens! Let your glory be over all the earth!"* (Psalm 108:5 ESV) Praise spreads the glory of God.

List several things you are thankful for. _____

_____

_____

Warning Siren – Day 28

By Craig Duck – President/Missionary

Read Proverbs 5

Encouragement for the day – *"My son, attend unto my wisdom, and bow thine ear to my understanding: That thou mayest regard discretion, and that thy lips may keep knowledge."*

Proverbs 5:1-2 KJV

There have been times when we have been fighting a fire and all of a sudden we will hear a lot of air horns and sirens. Around the same time evacuation tones will also be heard on the portable radios that we carry. When this happens, it is time to leave the building. Chiefs will typically choose to abandon the building because they do not like the progress that is being made or they have been given information from an officer on the interior recommending that units abandon the building. Either way, the building has become unsafe for units to be able to continue interior firefighting tactics. The other day we were listening to a fire online, and the evacuation tones went off. After several minutes it was apparent that one unit did not want to come out. When units disregard the warning siren, they put themselves in jeopardy of serious injury or even death.

God has given us valuable instruction in Proverbs chapter 5 through the Wisdom of Solomon. The evacuation tones are sounding, and it is time to leave the area. Those of us that are married need to read and reread this proverb. Solomon is encouraging us to get wisdom and to regard discretion. If we continue reading, we find that this Proverb is about married men avoiding the temptation to hang out with other women. Nothing good can come out of this situation. This path is a downward path that ultimately leads to one's death. God encourages us to love our wife and to guard her with everything we have. Hanging out with other women is equivalent to staying in a burning building after the chief has ordered the evacuation tones.

Lord, help me to love my wife. I thank you that you have provided her just for me. Help me to avoid hanging out with other women.

Encouraging first responders to keep the faith!!

Have You Ever Been Offended by a Coworker – Day 29
By Keith Helms – International Board Member and retired Battalion Fire Chief with the Charlotte Fire Department

Have you ever been offended by a coworker? Maybe you were falsely accused of an infraction or slandered in some way. How did you deal with the situation? While there is no step-by-step pattern of how we should react, the scriptures do give us some guidelines.

In Luke 6:27-36

Christ exhorts us to treat our offenders in the same manner that He did. ""But I say to you who are listening: Love your enemies, do good to those who hate you, bless those who curse you, pray for those who mistreat you. To the person who strikes you on the cheek, offer the other as well, and from the person who takes away your coat, do not withhold your tunic either. Give to everyone who asks you, and do not ask for your possessions back from the person who takes them away. Treat others in the same way that you would want them to treat you."

If you are confident and strong in your relationship with Christ, then you have the capacity to respond to offenses in a way that reflects the image of Christ and in a way that is in opposition to the world and the desires of your flesh. Turning the other cheek tells the offender that he/she is impotent to control your heart and mind. The offense hurts (just as a strike on the cheek) but the pain does not need to determine your thoughts or actions. Let the scriptures and the Holy Spirit direct your path. Also, when offended, make yourself accountable to a Christian brother who is not afraid to tell you when you are responding according to flesh, not the spirit.

For further study, begin with Romans 12:1-21

Notes:

_____

_____

_____

_____

_____

Pray Without Ceasing – Day 30

By Jonathan Williams – Firefighter with a large metro fire department in NC and FCFInternational Member

"With all prayer and petition pray at all times in the Spirit, and with this in view, be on the alert with all perseverance and petition for all the saints."

Ephesians 6:18, NASB

We are called to pray without ceasing in all circumstances and throughout each day of our lives. Developing a strong prayer life takes enormous discipline, as it is easily set aside due to the "busyness" that envelops our everyday lives. Subsequently, we must be resolute, we must schedule times of prayer and study so that they do not mindlessly get looked over throughout the course of the day. We must make prayer a priority in our lives in order to develop our personal walk and relationship with our Lord.

In all situations we are faced with the fact that we have two options:

1. We can try to handle the situation or problem on our own.

OR

2.	We can call on God, who is Omniscient (all-knowing), Omnipotent (all-powerful), and Omnipresent (ever-present, boundless).

Paul exhorts Christ-Followers, *"to be strong in the Lord and in the strength of His might".* (Eph. 6:10, NASB) We, alone, cannot do very much, because human effort is inadequate. Nevertheless, God, and His mighty power, is ample for us to effectively accomplish His will through our lives.

Today, take a moment to think of times that you could sit down, if only for five minutes, and devote that to prayer, to thanksgiving, to repentance, and to draw on God for His strength for those circumstances in which we most desperately need Him.

Notes:

_____

_____

_____

_____

Night Shift – Day 31

By Wayne Detzler – FCFInternational Board Member and Fire Chaplain (retired)

God sees the "night shift" of worship and ministry. Many times committed committee members gather at church to oversee the progress of God's work. And they usually do it after a hard day's work at their normal jobs. Some come off a commuter train, and others come straight from their local office, or from a hard day of teaching. Still they faithfully show up to guide us through the work of the Lord, or they welcome people into their home for hospitality. Recently we as elders met with the property and finance team for one purpose: prayer. Together we prayed for God's wisdom, as we move forward with the bold, audacious task of building a new worship home for Black Rock Congregational Church. The psalmist knew this, when he wrote:

"Oh, praise the LORD, all you servants of the LORD, you who serve at night in the house of the LORD. Lift up holy hands in prayer, and praise the LORD."

                                                    Psalm 134:1-2 NLT

As we praise and pray, God hears and answers those prayers.

Firehouse Dogs – Day 32

By Craig Duck – President/Missionary

Read Proverbs 12:1-10

Encouragement for the day – *"The righteous care for the needs of their animals, but the kindest acts of the wicked are cruel."*

Proverbs 12:10 NIV

There was a recent social media post that involved dogs in the firehouse. One of the local fire companies had adopted a firehouse dog, and they were proud to show it off to everyone. The problem came about when the fire chief found out. The department had a rule against animals in the firehouse, and he wanted the dog out. I am not sure what the outcome eventually became, but it is never good to be in a battle with the chief. Dogs have been in the fire service for a long time. Dalmatians helped to guide the horses to the fire and kept them calm along the way. I have seen firehouse dogs, cats, and even birds. There is something that draws firefighters to want to help animals.

Solomon was one of the wisest people to ever live. His writings in Proverbs have helped those who desire to please God for generations. Tucked away in chapter 12 this little verse talks about the ethical treatment of animals.

Righteous people, those who want to be remembered as pleasing God, care for the needs of all their animals. They don't abuse them or mistreat them. This very act is a picture of what God does for us. We don't deserve His love, yet He daily showers us with blessings and has taken us in to care for our needs. Wicked people, on the other hand, are cruel to their animals. All they care about is their selfish desires. They would never think to help anyone, let alone an animal, in their time of need. So, where do you line up with, the righteous or the wicked?

Lord, thank you for this reminder to care for those who need my help. May I encourage someone today who need hope.

Encouragement is the word of the day!!

Tough Stuff – Day 33

By Wayne Detzler – FCFInternational Board Member and Fire Chaplain (retired)

The Scripture teaches us a Jesus lesson: How to give away our lives. In His description of discipleship Jesus expanded the truth about giving. He taught us how to give away our very lives in service to others. Building on this concept the Apostle Paul wrote:

"And I will very gladly spend and be spent for your souls."
2 Cor. 12:15a NKJV

The commitment of Paul in penning this letter to his Corinthian friends is truly overwhelming. Then Paul adds this sad phrase: *"though the more abundantly I love you, the less I am loved."* (2 Cor. 12:15b NKJV) We do not love because others love us. We love because Jesus loves us. Is this tough stuff? Yes. But it is one of the marks of growing disciples.

In what ways have you been growing in your faith? _____

_____

_____

A Lonely Feeling – Day 34

By Craig Duck – President/Missionary

Read Deuteronomy 31:1-8

Encouragement for the day – *"It is the Lord who goes before you. He will be with you; he will not leave you or forsake you. Do not fear or be dismayed."*

                              Deuteronomy 31:8 ESV

The fire service can be a dangerous place to serve in. While it is always stressed to operate in teams of at least two, sometimes things can go wrong. Some line of duty deaths have occurred because one of the firefighters became separated from the crew and became lost. Such was the case with one of our firefighters operating on a large multi-dwelling apartment fire. This four-story ordinary constructed building had many void spaces, and the fire took advantage of that. The fire was growing quickly, and the incident commander ordered everyone out. One of the captains became lost during the process and sounded a mayday. Fortunately, we found him before it was too late. He told everyone that it was a lonely feeling. He sat down and waited for the end to come.

We are focused on a time when the Israelites are getting ready to cross into the promised land. Moses will not be joining them because God would not allow him to cross over. After Moses dies a new leader, Joshua, will lead them. At times of turmoil it is easy to become lonely. Moses was reassuring the folks that God will continue to lead them and will never leave them or forsake them. How comforting to know that this promise still holds true today. Many folks in the fire service become discouraged and lonely. They might be at the station with everyone around, but on the inside they feel lonely. We are reminded to run to God during those times and seek Him. As He led the Israelites to the promised land, He will lead you to victory over your trouble. Do not despair, God is on the move.

Lord, thank you for this reminder of just how much you love us. Give me strength to follow you no matter how difficult life becomes.

Encouragement should be a standard operating guideline!!

What is the Deepest Desire of Your Heart? – Day 35

By Keith Helms – International Board Member and retired Battalion Fire Chief with the Charlotte Fire Department

What is the deepest desire of your heart?

Without trying to come up with the "correct" answer, think about your deepest desire. Is it a good home life? A promotion? The approval and love of others? All of these can be good unless you never touch on a deeper desire; the desire for intimacy with God through Christ. When we fail to live for an ever-deepening relationship with God, then we will live for the lessor desires, opening the door to addictions. We will never be satisfied. We will continuously seek to find a way to numb the painful reality that life is not working for us. We will seek satisfaction in desires (legitimate and illegitimate) that were never intended to satisfy the core need of our heart. Pray that the Holy Spirit will open your heart to the most wonderful desire, the desire for Christ Himself. While we will not experience the complete fulfillment of intimacy with Christ until we are in heaven, what we can experience now is far superior to the temporary fulfillment of any other desire.

Search the scriptures to see if this is true. You can begin by studying these passages:

"for my people have committed two evils: they have forsaken me, the fountain of living waters, and hewed out cisterns for themselves, broken cisterns that can hold no water."
Jeremiah 2:13 ESV

"As a deer pants for flowing streams, so pants my soul for you, O God."
Psalm 42:1 ESV

"Come, everyone who thirsts, come to the waters; and he who has no money, come, buy and eat! Come, buy wine and milk without money and without price. Why do you spend your money for that which is not bread, and your labor for that which does not satisfy? Listen diligently to me, and eat what is good, and delight yourselves in rich food."
Isaiah 55:1-2 ESV

Also check out Psalm 28, Psalm 63, and Philippians 3:7-21

Door Control – Day 36

By Andrew Starnes – Battalion Chief with a large metro department in NC and FCFInternational Member

A door that no one can close

In the fire service today, it is alive with research, development, and forward-thinking leaders helping to bring positive change to the world.

One such topic is Anti-Ventilation.

By controlling the fires air flow, we thereby control its growth. As firefighters, we often start off our fire service journey as free burning "fuel regulated" fires that seem inextinguishable.

But then life happens:

Our passion for what we do becomes choked down by negativity, amount of other fires we have burning (too many commitments) and need more air (encouragement, time, and energy). We have become vent limited; our 'fire' has reached a decay phase. We have let others that are too weak to follow their own dreams discourage ours.

Consider this:

"Ask and it will be given to you, seek and you will find; knock and the door will be opened to you. For everyone asks receives; the one who seeks finds, and the one who knocks the door will be opened"

Matthew 7:7-8 NIV

Remember, that as we journey through the fires of our lives when all other doors are closed, one remains open, the door into the presence of God through prayer. Force the door open with the most powerful forcible entry tool there is:

Prayer

How much time throughout the day are you actively engaged in meaningful prayer? _____

_____

How often do you immediately stop and prayer for someone who has asked you to pray for them? _____

_____

Molding Our Lives – Day 37

By Wayne Detzler – FCFInternational Board Member and Fire Chaplain (retired)

"If it is true that you look favorably on me, let me know your ways so I may understand you more fully and continue to enjoy your favor." Moses cried out to the Lord, and the LORD (Yahweh) replied, 'I will personally go with you, Moses, and I will give you rest—everything will be fine for you.'"

Exodus 33:13-14 NLT

Moses craved assurance from Yahweh, and the Lord gave it to him. The Lord always answers our prayer, when we cry out to Him. And as He answers, He molds our lives more and more into the likeness of the Lord Jesus Christ.

In what ways has God answered your prayers in the past?

_____

_____

_____

Take Some Leave Some – Day 38
By Craig Duck – President/Missionary

Read Proverbs 15:20-29

Encouragement for the day – *"Whoever is greedy for unjust gain troubles his own household, but he who hates bribes will live."*

Proverbs 15:27 ESV

The first time I heard the phrase "take some leave some" I was sitting in a firehouse in Washington, DC. The cook for the day had just come in and told everyone that he had laid out short. For whatever reason, he hadn't bought enough food at the grocery store and was afraid we were going to run out of food. He knew that firefighters love to eat and can easily devour more calories in a meal than most citizens do in a day or two. By saying "take some leave some," he was hoping everyone would be mindful of others in line behind them and not be so greedy with their portion.

The Bible talks a lot about greed. The problem with greed is we can effortlessly be consumed with a desire to want more stuff and find ourselves making poor choices to get it. As we become devoured by greed, we ultimately cause reel physical harm to our families. This desire for things will lead us to a point where we become slaves to the world. We rise early, stay up late, take on more jobs, and even begin to cheat to acquire all the things we must have. Before we know it, we can quickly gain money by illegal means and disgrace our family name. Christian firefighters and first responders need to focus on being content (Hebrews 13:5). Rather than pursuing money and things, we need to focus on pleasing God and serving Him. When your life is over, what will you be remembered for? A person who loved money, or one who loved God.

Lord, help me not to be distracted today. May I focus all my efforts on pleasing you in the department you have called me to.

Encouragement is designed to be shared with others!!

Know Your Enemy – Day 39

By Jonathan Riffe – FCFInternational Member

When General George Patton counterattacked Field Marshal Rommel in World War II, Patton is reported to have shouted in the thick of battle, "I read your book, Rommel! I read your book!" Patton had studied Rommel's Infantry Attacks.

We can know the same about the Devil.

We know Satan will attack weak spots first. Forty days of fasting left Jesus famished, so Satan began with the topic of bread. Jesus' stomach was empty, so to the stomach Satan turned. Where are you empty? Bring your weaknesses to God before Satan brings them to you.

"So that Satan will not outsmart us. For we are familiar with his evil schemes."

2 Corinthians 2:11 NLT

Lord help me today to follow all your ways. May the enemy not have an opportunity to hold me back from serving you.

Honor His Word – Day 40

John Epps – FCFInternational Member

If you Love the Lord, you will Honor His Word, you will Keep His Word and you will Lean on His Word.

The King Is Coming!

"But whoso keepeth his word, in him verily is the love of God perfected: hereby know we that we are in him."

1 John 2:5 KJV

In what ways have you been dishonoring the Lord at your station?

What does it mean to keep God's Word?

List several ways you can obey the truths of the Bible?

The Next Generation – Day 41

By Craig Duck – President/Missionary

Read Deuteronomy 6:1-9

Encouragement for the day – *"You shall teach them diligently to your children, and shall talk of them when you sit in your house, when you walk by the way, when you lie down, and when you rise up."*

Deuteronomy 6:7 NKJV

Most firefighters and first responders love the fire service. You see this in the dedication and commitment that they have to their departments and the communities in which they serve. Some families have multiple generations serving in the same department, and you can see the love that they have for serving. Who doesn't get excited when they see a father passing on the knowledge of firefighting to his son or daughter? I remember riding the tailboard of a fire truck with my dad and the discussions we had about firefighting. These early days instilled a sense of commitment to the department we served in and a great love for the job. I would not be the firefighter I am today without my dad's help and instruction.

Christian first responders are encouraged to pass on a great love for God to their children. In today's passage of the Bible, the Israelites are preparing to cross into the Promised Land. Before they cross over, God is giving them instructions for the next generation. As you read through this passage in the Bible, notice the parent's responsibilities. First, they are to love God with all their heart and develop an intimate relationship with Him. Then they are to pass this love on to their children. Just like the firefighter who takes every opportunity to teach the younger generation, so too we are to take every opportunity to teach our children about God. In so doing we will not only change our lives but our children's as well. Whole communities can be altered for the better as people learn to put the needs of others before their own needs.

Lord, help me today to share the great love I have with You to my children.

Making encouragement a priority makes sense!!

Obligation – Day 42

By Wayne Detzler – FCFInternational Board Member and Fire Chaplain (retired)

"For I have a great sense of obligation to people in both the civilized world and the rest of the world, to the educated and uneducated alike."

Rom. 1:14 NLT

Paul took his role as a witness very seriously. He spoke of it as an "obligation," and this continually amazes me. The God of the universe chooses people like us to be His witness on this earth. Jesus says, we are lights in a dark world. (Matt. 5:16) So, wherever we are, let's shine for Jesus today.

How have you been a light in a dark world this past week?

_____

_____

If you have not been faithful in sharing the Gospel message with others, how can you better prepare to be good at that skill?

Bullying in the Fire Service – Day 43
By Craig Duck – President/Missionary

Read Psalm 19

Encouragement for the day – *"Let the words of my mouth, and the meditation of my heart, be acceptable in thy sight, O Lord, my strength, and my redeemer."*

Psalm 19:14 KJV

As I sat in the breakfast area of a hotel eating a banana when the news caught my attention. When I had left for FDIC a young firefighter from Virginia was missing and a search was on. Sadly, they had located the body of this firefighter and an investigation into her death was beginning. The news story was reporting a possible reason; it appeared that this firefighter had committed suicide. The reporter went on to explain that this might be an awful case of bullying. Several comments had been made on an anonymous website that might give investigators a clue in the case. I sat and reflected on how horrible this story was and how saddened the family and department must be. I began to reflect on the problem of bullying in the fire service.

The words we choose to use can either encourage or discourage someone. Christian firefighters and first responders need to think before they speak when it comes to talking to other firefighters. This can be difficult sometimes, but it is crucial that we only use words that will lift people up and provide them with comfort and hope. The Psalmist reminds us that we are accountable to God for every word we choose to use, and even our thoughts. Some of us have to work very hard at selecting the right words to say to some firefighters in our department, but it is critical that we find the right ones. Don't worry; God will give you the right words to say when you need them if you commit all of your ways to Him. Firefighters today are under a lot of stress in the fire service; let's not add to that stress. May our words greatly encourage those we come in contact with today.

Lord thank you for reminding me today to choose my words carefully. May you be glorified as I encourage others today.

Encouragement is the art of picking people up when they are down!!

Which is More Important – Day 44

By Keith Helms – International Board Member and retired Battalion Fire Chief with the Charlotte Fire Department

Consider This Question

Which is more important? A ladder co. or an engine co.? Truth or love?

One of the entertaining facets at a two-piece station is the rivalry between the engine and ladder companies. Both companies go to great extremes to prove that they are more important at a working fire. In the banter which occurs after the incident, both companies will brag about everything that they did, and they will minimize what the others did. Which one is right? Is it the engine company or the ladder company that does most of the critical work at a fire? The obvious answer is that both companies are critical to the successful control of a structure fire. Both rely on the other. Both are essential.

There is a similar debate in Christianity today. Which is more important from a scriptural basis...truth and doctrine or love and relationships? Many churches today are very strong in one and weak in the other. One is emphasized and the other is all but ignored. However, the spiritually healthy church focuses equally on both. Like the two sides of a coin, truth and love are the complementary sides of a healthy church. Truth without love results in arrogant Pharisees, people more interested in being right than being like Christ. Love without truth results in shallow, immature believers who just want everyone (especially themselves) to feel good. The scriptures are abundant in convicting passages that stress the need to teach clear doctrine that results in a transformed life; a life that reflects the image of Christ and loves as He loved.

Just as a ladder company and engine company are complementary, so are truth and love. They were never meant to be separated.

"And this I pray, that your love may abound still more and more in knowledge and all discernment, that you may approve the things that are excellent, that you may be sincere and without offense till the day of Christ, being filled with the fruits of righteousness which are by Jesus Christ, to the glory and praise of God."

Philippians 1:9-11 NKJV

No Situation too Great – Day 45

By Jonathan Williams – Firefighter with a large metro fire department in NC and FCFInternational Member

"And pray on my behalf, that utterance may be given to me in the opening of my mouth, to make known with boldness the mystery of the gospel, for which I am an ambassador in chains; that in proclaiming it I may speak boldly, as I ought to speak."

Ephesians 6:19-20, NASB

Most of us, if not all of us, when confronted with hard times or unfortunate circumstances, we want to free ourselves from them swiftly. We do not like to be in situations that cause us harm, discomfort, or cause us to struggle. Yet, this was precisely the situation that Paul was in when he wrote this letter to the Ephesians, he was in prison.

It is very encouraging, and a little surprising, that Paul, even though he was imprisoned for his beliefs, didn't request the church to pray to God for his release. Consequently, he asked that the Christians in Ephesus to pray for him to be capable of effectively proclaiming the Gospel message both clearly and fearlessly whenever and wherever the opportunity presented itself. Despite the known and unknown consequences of proclaiming the

Gospel, which happened to be why he was in prison to begin with, he aspired to do nothing else but to continue to fulfill the calling in which God had placed on his life, to proclaim the Gospel to the Gentile nation.

In general, this should encourage us as Christ-Followers to see how God is able to use us, no matter where we are in life, or what circumstances we may be in. It, in effect, should encourage us to trust that God is able to work His will through us wherever we are, or whatever stage of life we are in. Paul was in prison, yet he was still following through with his calling by leading those who were far away from Christ into a relationship with Him, regardless of what circumstances befell him on the way.

No situation or circumstance is too great, or too adverse, that God is not able to use us for His will. What may appear to be a lost hope, or a dead end to a never-ending situation, God has a divine will that usurp all things. As you go through difficult times, trust God and His will for your life, trusting that He has a plan, and that you have a calling, through which God is able to work through those particular situations to His ultimate glory.

It All comes down to trusting in God.

Suicide on the Installment Plan – Day 46

By Andrew Starnes – Battalion Chief with a large metro department in NC and FCFInternational Member

"Without realizing it, we often carry something around with us everywhere we go. We bring it out in our conversations, and it shows up in our attitudes. It never really existed, yet it's power lives among us and keeps us from moving forward." Author unknown.

Many times, we overlook the distant look in a fellow firefighter's eyes. Slowly, with the constant assault on our heart we begin to die on the inside. It begins with a look, an act of omission, choosing to remove oneself, and the very lines on our face can tell more than many of us would like to admit about the condition of our heart.

We blindly and foolishly believe that we can move through our days and function without others realizing that we are silently suffering on the inside. Our behaviors give us away and cry out to others what our prideful selves refuse to do. We are showing signs of a tremendous fire inside our hearts, slowly burning, choked down but not out.

In these moments, if not careful, we can hurt others in so many ways. We push others away and build walls around our hearts.
We seal off our emotions as if they were a hazardous material that no one should touch.

Yet in reality, we have been hurt so deeply that we would rather suffer in solitude than allow anyone else into our world that may hurt us again.

But do we realize that our defensive efforts are actually destructive ones to others and ourselves?

Do we really want to spend our lives pushing others away?

Do we realize what we are doing to others by 'protecting' ourselves?

If we are not careful, we are leading others down the same dark path as we assume our defensive posture.

What can we do?

We cannot continue nor allow others to suffer alone. We must not let these brothers or sisters think that no one cares for them. They are carrying a sign around their neck that is printed in bold letters:

"HELP ME!"

Those who suffer in this way experience a slow and gradual death. It is suicide on the installment plan. Day by day a piece of them dies right in front of the world yet no one says or does anything about it. Will we as leaders, friends, and believers take the time to speak words of comfort?

Will we take the time to listen to them?
Will we take the time to care?
Will we be so focused on saving lives that we fail to save the lives that are dying right in front of us?
Will we shine His light into their darkness?

Jesus said, *"I am the light of the world. Whoever follows me will never walk in darkness but will have the light of life."*

John 8:12 NIV

For if we don't take the time, we may live the regret of the results of their collateral damage, either theirs or our wasted life, or the memories of what we should have done to try to help.

Let us ask ourselves
Would we want to be treated as they are being treated?
Don't we realize that their behaviors are a cry for help?
Who will help them?

We save others but yet we are failing to save ourselves...

As leaders we cannot ignore their silent cries that says more than words can ever say. We cannot ignore them no more than a person hanging from a fiery window screaming for help.

Those that we know who carry these burdens are trapped at a fiery window and only those in their fellowship, those closest to them, will be able to make the rescue if they act in time.

Take the time to share Jesus with them. Be the brother or sister that they need when the call comes in. Don't wait, respond and make the greatest rescue: The rescue of a broken life. Give them the greatest gift that you can give: The gift or your compassionate presence. You will never regret it.

Ringing in My Ears – Day 47

By Wayne Detzler – FCFInternational Board Member and Fire Chaplain (retired)

"Praise his name with dancing, accompanied by tambourine and harp. For the LORD delights in his people; he crowns the humble with victory.

Psalm 149:3-4 NKJV

Early in the morning I read and meditated on this encouraging psalm. A picture popped into my memory. It is the large and thriving house church in Xuchang, China, where Margaret and I had the privilege of serving as co-preachers. The joyful worship rings in my ears to this day. And the good news is this, God rejoices when we worship exuberantly.

What kind of songs do you regularly listen to and sing along with? _____

_____

What type of music does God dislike? _____

_____

Don't Tell Them Show Them – Day 48
By Craig Duck – President/Missionary

Read John 3:16-21

Encouragement for the day – *"For God so loved the world that He gave His only begotten Son, that whoever believes in Him should not perish but have everlasting life."*

John 3:16 NKJV

I recently saw an article in a fire service trade magazine that was titled "Don't tell them show them." This article went on to encourage firefighters and first responders to not only tell others of ways to be a good firefighter but to show them how to do it. Anyone can stand in front of a group of first responders and teach a class. But do they live out what they teach on the fireground? Do their actions match what they tell others to do? The great instructors do. Their life is an open book where folks who make a study of them quickly learn what it takes to be a successful firefighter.

Jesus Christ was the utmost example of this principle that ever lived. He not only showed His disciples how to live a life that is pleasing to God; He demonstrated it to us as well. Jesus demonstrated to the world what love is all about. Jesus healed the sick, raised the dead, fed the hungry, preached the kingdom, cast out demons, and gave His life in love for the world. This was real love in action. No other religion can measure up to what God accomplished at the cross of Calvary. Sins forgiven and relationships restored because of Jesus. He didn't just tell us how to please God; He showed us. Because of Jesus we now have access to God the Father in a way that we never thought possible before we surrendered to Him.

Lord, thank you for saving my soul. Give me courage today to share this message with the rest of the fire service.

Encouragement should be a standard operating guideline!!

Feeling Unappreciated – Day 49

By Andrew Starnes – Battalion Chief with a large metro department in NC and FCFInternational Member

Down, and not Valued? Consider This

Every day that you decide to smile in the face of adversity you will unknowingly lift someone else's spirit. Every day you choose to serve the impoverished, the addict, the homeless with compassion and love you make a difference. Every day you choose to do the hard work of being honest instead of taking the easy way out you have sown a seed in another's heart of what integrity truly means.

Every day that you work out instead of lying on the couch and complaining you set the example.

Every day that you read, train, and mentor others you make an impact on their future for the moment and for their lifetime. Every day that you bow your head and pray you show others that your allegiance goes to a higher calling than any badge can bestow. Every day that you take the time to listen to your brother/sister, who is struggling, you show what it truly means to "carry each other's burdens" (Galatians 6:2).

Every day that you refuse to fall victim to bitterness you will lead without even knowing. Every day that you put your faith and your family first over all other commitments, you are teaching others how to prioritize their lives.

Many would stop at this point and say but "Why me?"

Do not underestimate the power of your influence, your encouragement, and your compassion for others. When the world tells you that you can't make a difference pick up a Bible and read. Read about all the men and women who faced insurmountable circumstances, but God showed his mighty power through them. Read about Paul (a mentor), Barnabas (an encourager), and Timothy (a disciple). Surround yourself with individuals like these.

Read about Jesus and how he loved in spite of circumstances and how he led in the face of adversity. Read about how He prayed with great anguish when he was dismayed. Read and see how He had compassion on the sick, the imprisoned, the homeless, the widow, and the orphan. Read about how He did all of this not for the world's recognition but out of God's great love for you.

If you want to make a difference, if you want to renew your passion, and if you want to truly help others; welcome back to your calling. Call upon God. He will give you the strength that you desire.

"I can do all things through Christ who strengthens me"
                                              Philippians 4:13 NIV

And if you believe that you can't share your passionate beliefs at work think again. And let your profession be your pulpit as *"whatever you do, whether in word or deed, do it all in the name of the Lord Jesus, giving thanks to God the Father through Him."* (Colossians 3:17)

Be encouraged this day and know that God is making a difference through you each and every day.

When was the last time you picked up your Bible and read it? _____

_____

How much time each day do you devote to reading your Bible? _____

Rocks Cry Out – Day 50

By John Epps – FCFInternational Member

Don't let the rocks cry and sing in your place, sing and make a joyful noise!

The King Is Coming!

"O come, let us sing unto the Lord : let us make a joyful noise to the rock of our salvation. Let us come before his presence with thanksgiving, and make a joyful noise unto him with psalms."

Psalms 95:1-2 KJV

Why do you think the Psalmist chose to use the words "rock of our salvation" in Psalm 95?

Do you believe that rocks will literally sing in our place if we choose not to sing praises to God?

When Hope Lies Buried – Day 51

By Wayne Detzler – FCFInternational Board Member and Fire Chaplain (retired)

"Afterward Joseph of Arimathea, who had been a secret disciple of Jesus (because he feared the Jewish leaders), asked Pilate for permission to take down Jesus' body. When Pilate gave permission, Joseph came and took the body away. With him came Nicodemus, the man who had come to Jesus at night."

John 19:38-39 NLT

They buried Jesus and assumed that it was all over. But Jesus promised He would rise from the dead.

Let's never let circumstances blind us to the promises of God.

How has God answered your prayers in the past? _____

_____

Why is it so difficult to trust in God when you are walking through difficult times? _____

_____

Everyone Goes Home – Day 52

By Craig Duck – President/Missionary

Read I John 5:6-12

Encouragement for the day – *"The one who has the Son has life. The one who doesn't have the Son of God does not have life."*

I John 5:12 HCSB

In 2004 the National Fallen Firefighters Foundation (NFFF) launched an initiative that they hoped would change the fire service. The initiatives goal was to reduce the number of preventable firefighter fatalities. Respected leaders met together to find ways to meet the goals of the program. The group came up with 16 initiatives and offered top-level training to ensure that everyone goes home. Sadly, some departments are unaware of the initiatives, and still, others refuse to implement the 16 initiatives.

God has implemented His own initiative that firefighters and first responders can take advantage. Due to the sin problem that has affected all people since the original sin of Adam back in Genesis chapter 3, man has been unable to have an eternal relationship with God. God dispatched His Son Jesus Christ to the earth to pay the penalty for our sins and establish that eternal relationship with Him. Jesus was able to accomplish this task because He came to the earth, lived a perfect life and died to pay the penalty for our sins. Jesus has risen from the dead and is now sitting at the right hand of God where He is interceding for His own. Like the 16 initiatives of NFFF, most firefighters today disregard God's plan and try to make it on their own. What hinders you today from coming to God, asking forgiveness of your sins and trusting in the Son of God to deliver you out of bondage? If you would like to learn more on this subject, please visit our website to find the answers.

www.fellowshipofchristianfirefighters.org

Lord thank you for your free gift of eternal life through Jesus Christ our lord. Give me courage today to share His great redemptive story with others.

Encouragement is the art of lifting others up when they are down!!

Sovereign Grace O'er Sin Abounding – Day 53

By Wayne Detzler – FCFInternational Board Member and Fire Chaplain (retired)

"Wait on the Lord, And keep His way, And He shall exalt you to inherit the land; When the wicked are cut off, you shall see it."

Psalm 37:34 NKJV

This psalm urges patience, as we wait for the Lord to work. During the past election cycle, accusations of evil grieved my soul. Then I began to realize that the Lord is and will be in charge—even when public evil runs rampant. King David concludes: *"But the salvation of the righteous is from the Lord; He is their strength in the time of trouble. And the Lord shall help them and deliver them; He shall deliver them from the wicked, And save them, Because they trust in Him."* (Psalm 37:39-40 NKJV)

Why is it so easy to get caught up in political drama? _____

_____

Where should our focus be? _____

_____

Rekindle – Day 54
By Craig Duck – President/Missionary

Read Revelation 2:1-7

Encouragement for the day – *"Yet I hold this against you: You have forsaken the love you had at first."*

Revelation 2:4 NIV

Most fire chiefs do not like to hear the word "rekindle." By definition, a rekindle is a fire that occurs in a tenable building up to eight hours after the last company leaves the scene and is determined by the investigators to be an extension of the original fire. Rekindles make your department look bad because you were not able to fully extinguish the fire and it damages more of the structure than it should have. To ensure that a fire won't rekindle it is important to open up around the fire area until you reach unburned wood. We had a lieutenant years ago that would take one last look around after all the hose was repacked on the apparatus and we were ready to leave. We never had a rekindle as long as that lieutenant was working.

For the Christian firefighter and first responder the term "rekindle" is used oppositely and is considered good not bad. As life gets so busy, we sometimes forget to spend quality time with God. In the fire service, we get busy with training, going to emergencies and filling out reports. For firefighters with families, there are ball games, schoolwork, and parties to attend. Before you know it there is no time left for God. In Revelation, we learn that the church at Ephesus is getting judged for their lack of commitment to God. While God commends them for their labor and their commitment (2:2), they are then reminded that they have left their first love. As you evaluate your commitment to God today, resolve to rekindle your love for Him. Rekindling your love for God takes time and energy that is focused on Him. Even though your life is busy, remember to carve out enough time to devote to the God who loves you more than life itself.

Lord, forgive me for not spending time with You, help me today to give you the honor and respect that You deserve and teach me how to live a life that is pleasing to You.

Encouragement should be a standard in every department!!

It's OK to Doubt – Day 55

By Wayne Detzler – FCFInternational Board Member and Fire Chaplain (retired)

"Crossing bridges before I get to them," or "Jumping to conclusions." It's the only exercise I get some days. But the good news is this--God knows I am weak and that I doubt sometimes. Jesus' earthly brother wrote these helpful words:

"But you, beloved, building yourselves up in your most holy faith and praying in the Holy Spirit, keep yourselves in the love of God, waiting for the mercy of our Lord Jesus Christ that leads to eternal life. And have mercy on those who doubt."

Jude 20-22 ESV

Why can it be easy to doubt what God says? _____

_____

What will you do this week to ensure you will not doubt what God has said in His Word? _____

_____

Attention All Units and Stations Concerned Day 56

By Craig Duck – President/Missionary

Read Ecclesiastes 9:11-17

Encouragement for the day – *"Moreover, no one knows when their hour will come: As fish are caught in a cruel net, or birds are taken in a snare, so people are trapped by evil times that fall unexpectedly upon them."*

Ecclesiastes 9:12 NIV

When I first became a firefighter for the District of Columbia Fire Department every firehouse had a vocal alarm system. This system was designed to alert companies of a call and give them any pertinent information. The vocal alarm system was a small box that had a speaker and a microphone. Located in the watch room, firefighters could listen to all the alarms that were dispatched in the city or communicate with the dispatchers. Before every message that was put out over the vocal alarm system, the dispatcher would say "attention all units and stations concerned." This little statement reminded us to stop what we were doing and listen to the message.

Has God ever tried to get your attention? Maybe things aren't going your way at the station. Perhaps you wrecked the fire truck or were hurt at a fire. Maybe God is trying to tell you that you are on the wrong road. You are self-centered and don't care about the things of God. You might have recently been involved with another firefighter's death, and you realize that life is short. We as firefighters and first responders think we are invincible, but that is simply not the case. Don't wait until later to have a relationship with Christ. Turn to God today and begin obeying the truth in the Bible. God loves you and desires to forgive your sins. Take a moment right now and ask God to be the Lord of your life, forgiving you of the sins you have committed.

Lord, thank you for your salvation, so rich and so free. May I have the wisdom to know how to share it with others.

Encouraging firefighters and first responders to keep the faith!!

What Difference Does Your Faith Make? – Day 57

By Keith Helms – International Board Member and retired Battalion Fire Chief with the Charlotte Fire Department

Believing in Jesus Christ as your savior changes your eternal destination. Your faith in Christ (or lack of faith) determines whether you will spend eternity in heaven or hell. But what about today? Does my faith in Christ make a difference in my life today? In 1 Timothy 4:8, we read "…for while bodily training is of some value, godliness is of value in every way, as it holds promise for the present life and also for the life to come." So how does our relationship with the Lord affect our lives now? Primary, it is seen in the context of relationships. First, we now have a relationship with the Lord that can be deep and intimate. Our appetite for intimacy with God can and should be the primary desire of our heart. Psalm 73:28 tells us "But for me it is good to be near God; I have made the Lord God my refuge, that I may tell of all your works." Similarly, Psalm 42:1 says, "As the deer pants for the water brooks, So pants my soul for You, O God." Second, our faith can and should have an effect on our relationships with others. Read Galatians 5:22-23 where Paul presents the fruit of the Spirit; eight characteristics that are all foundationally relational. A faith that is growing and active will always be evidenced in fruit-bearing relationships.

Is your faith making a difference in your life today? Examine your relationship with the Lord; examine your relationships with others (especially those within your immediate family). Remember that Christ said that all of Law and the Prophets hang on two commandments: Love God and love others (Matthew 22:36-40). Work diligently to work out your faith in the context of relationships. God will be glorified.

For additional study, begin with these passages:
- 2 Peter 1:5-11
- James 2:14-26
- Colossians 3

Notes:

Real Worship – Day 58

By Wayne Detzler – FCFInternational Board Member and Fire Chaplain (retired)

"Holy, holy, holy is the Lord God, the Almighty— the one who always was, who is, and who is still to come."

Revelation 4:8 NLT

We all want to worship the Lord better, and the Scripture gives us clues. This is one of the songs sung in heaven, and it focuses on the holiness of God. Notice the absence of any reference to us as worshippers in the song, the entire emphasis is on the God we praise and worship. The heavenly worshipers continue with this song: *"You are worthy, O Lord our God, to receive glory and honor and power. For you created all things, and they exist because you created what you pleased."* (Revelation 4:11 NLT)

Let's practice this kind of worship here and now!

In what practical ways can you better worship God this week? _____

_____

Defensible Space – Day 59

By Craig Duck – President/Missionary

Read I Peter 3:13-22

Encouragement for the day – *"But in your hearts honor Christ the Lord as holy, always being prepared to make a defense to anyone who asks you for a reason for the hope that is in you; yet do it with gentleness and respect,"*

I Peter 3:15 ESV

Defensible space is a relatively new term in the fire service and is used primarily out west. Creating defensible space around your home is critical to the survival of your home during a wildfire. The bigger the fire can become; the better chances are that your house will not survive the fire. If the homeowners allow vegetation and ignitable material to accumulate near the house, it is easier for the fire to spread. It is hard to defend your property if you haven't prepared it before the fire occurs. Some departments will even go around their district and ensure that residents are ready for fire season.

Christian firefighters and first responders live in a world where many different religions are promoted. You can quickly become confused on what is truth and what is not. It is mission critical that every Christian firefighter and first responder understand what the Bible says. Before we are confronted by other people, we should have a good grasp of Biblical principles. This takes time and effort on our part. We cannot learn what God says if we leave our Bibles on the shelf collecting dust. Daily we must take it out to read and study what it has to say. Then when someone in our department asks for the reason of the hope that is in us, we will be ready to give an answer. If others challenge our faith, we will also be able to defend it with gentleness and respect.

Lord, give me a desire today to read and study my Bible. May I learn something about you that I did not know before.

Encouraging firefighters and first responders to keep the faith!!

Holding the Line – Day 60

By Andrew Starnes – Battalion Chief with a large metro department in NC and FCFInternational Member

Who's your true back-up?

"Therefore a man shall leave his father and mother and hold fast to his wife, and the two shall become one flesh."
                                        Ephesians 5:31 ESV

Firefighters understand the value of teamwork. We are taught from the very beginning that the success of our efforts is based upon how well we work together. One of the areas that this is most evident is during hose-line advancement.

The end result of the nozzle man's work of extinguishment is directly correlated to how well the backup firefighter works with them. In short, without the back-up firefighter working in unison, anticipating the next move, pulling the weight, and working out the kinks; the nozzle man's job would be very difficult if not impossible.

As firefighters, the value of teamwork is so instrumental to what we do that the following statistic is contradictory to everything we stand for:

Firefighters have the highest percentage of divorce than any other profession. (Between 60-84%)

If the success of our efforts in firefighting is based on how well we work together, then shouldn't the success of our efforts at work be based on those holding the line for us at home?

As I have just returned from a week of some of the most invigorating and inspirational time with some of the greatest fire service minds in the world, I would like to take a moment and give thanks for my wife. While I was teaching, learning, and growing in my understanding of fire behavior she was at home holding the line by herself. She took care of our daughter, took care of the house, took care of the bills, cleaned, cooked, and had to face being cooped up due to the snowstorm.

The point is this; behind every successful man is the foundation of a strong, loving, and hardworking wife. I owe my life and everything in it to the grace of God. Because of His great love, He saved me through Jesus and has given me a glimpse of true unconditional love in the person of my wife.

Dear friends, if you are married, I write this message to you today as a reminder that while you may face great trials in your job your spouse is "holding the line" anticipating your next move, working in unison, and advancing the line all alone.

The next time you are inside fighting a fire and everything goes smoothly due to the work of your team, remember that team member at home who is holding the line alone for you.

Notes:

_____

_____

_____

_____

_____

The Holy Spirit Gives Victory over Temptation – Day 61
By Wayne Detzler – FCFInternational Board Member and Fire Chaplain (retired)

For many years I have been studying, writing, teaching, and counseling in the area of spiritual victory. More important, I have been learning daily how to overcome temptations. This spiritual warfare never ends—young and old have their own battles. But ALL have battles. So, the teaching of St. Paul is extremely important:

"If you live under the power of sin, you will die. But by the Spirit's power you can put to death the sins you commit. Then you will live. Those who are led by the Spirit of God are children of God."

Romans 8:13-14 NIRV

Victorious Lord, for myself and for those I love, please lead us each and all in spiritual victory this day. Amen.

In what ways are you tempted in the fire service to commit sins? _____

_____

_____

Spinning Wheels – Day 62

By Craig Duck – President/Missionary

Read Malachi 1:6-14

Encouragement for the day – *"A son honors his father, and a servant his master. If then I am a father, where is my honor? And if I am a master, where is my fear? says the Lord of hosts to you, O priests, who despise my name. But you say, 'How have we despised your name?'"*

Malachi 1:6 ESV

This fall and winter there has been a lot of rain in our area. Since many of our roads are still dirt roads, it makes driving apparatus on calls very interesting. Many of the fire trucks have been stuck in the mud and needed to get towed out to make it back to the firehouse. Those firefighters and first responders in the north and west have had a large amount of snow and have times when their apparatus has become stuck as well. It is always bad as a driver to put the vehicle in drive only to spin the wheels and go nowhere.

Today we are in the last book of the Old Testament. Malachi is a prophet whose name means "My Messenger." God sent Malachi to the people of Israel because evidently, they we just going through the motions and not truly worshipping God. The people were giving sacrifices that didn't meet the requirements and were unacceptable to Him. They were just spinning their wheels and not going anywhere in their spiritual life. How often do we do something similar in our worship to God? Sure, we might attend church, read our Bible, and tell others about Jesus but have we become complacent in our attitudes toward God. God desires us to give our best to Him, not just our leftovers. Our walk with Christ should readily show others what He has done in our life and the thankfulness we have for being pulled out of the mire pit.

May our actions and attitudes today be pleasing to you, oh Lord. May my sacrifices honor your great name.

Encouragement goes a long way when shared with others!!

Dressing a Wound – Day 63

By Craig Duck – President/Missionary

Read Psalm 147

Encouragement for the day – *"He heals the brokenhearted and binds up their wounds."*

Psalm 147:3 ESV

Many fire departments in America provide emergency medical services to the citizens in their district. One of the many tasks that firefighters will regularly have to do is dress a wound. Whether the injuries were caused by gunshot wounds, motor vehicle accidents, or industrial mishaps, today's firefighters must be prepared for anything. The bleeding must be stopped, and the wound covered to help prevent infection. Placing four by fours on the injury and wrapping them with cling is common in today's fire service. While this doesn't sound glamorous, it helps to save lives.

There are many people in the fire service who are hurting. Their wounds are deep, and they have lost all hope. Perhaps you have been wounded by a loved one, lost out on a promotion, or made a terrible mistake. The Psalmist encourages those who are brokenhearted to run to God. Only He is powerful enough to put your broken pieces back together. Verse 11 reminds us that; "the Lord takes pleasure in those who fear him, in those who hope in his steadfast love." God can restore relationships and return you to a place of peace and mercy. Don't let the world steer you away from God. Run to Him and allow the Almighty to do a great work in your life today.

Lord, thank you for your eternal love for me. Help me to cling to you when my world seems to be falling apart.

Encouraging firefighters and first responders to keep the faith!!

Willis Watkins – Day 64

By Keith Helms – International Board Member and retired Battalion Fire Chief with the Charlotte Fire Department

Early in my career, I was assigned to Ladder 2. The engineer was Willis Watkins, a great man of few words. He listened more than he spoke, however when he did speak, everyone listened. Typically, his words would end a discussion since even the captains were wise enough not to challenge him. The book of Proverbs has many passages that describe the wisdom of a man who has learned to tame the tongue.

Willis is a wise man who lived out these tongue tamers. I encourage you to do the same.

Proverbs' Tongue Tamers:

Proverbs 10:19   "When words are many, transgression is not lacking, but whoever restrains his lips is prudent."

Proverbs 17:27-28   "Whoever restrains his words has knowledge, and he who has a cool spirit is a man of understanding. Even a fool who keeps silent is considered wise; when he closes his lips, he is deemed intelligent."

Proverbs 18:2   *"A fool takes no pleasure in understanding, but only in expressing his opinion."*

Proverbs 18:8   *"The words of a gossip are like choice morsels; they go down to a man's inmost parts."*

Proverbs 18:13   *"If one gives an answer before he hears, it is his folly and shame."*

Proverbs 18:21   *"Death and life are in the power of the tongue, and those who love it will eat its fruits."*

Proverbs 21:23   *"Whoever keeps his mouth and his tongue keeps himself out of trouble."*

Proverbs 29:20   *"Do you see a man who is hasty in his words? There is more hope for a fool than for him."*

For further study on taming the tongue, read the following:

Psalm 19:14; Matthew 12:36-37; Matthew 15:7-20; Ephesians 4:29; Colossians 4:6; James 3:5-10; 1 Peter 3:10

Propelled by Passion – Day 65

By Wayne Detzler – FCFInternational Board Member and Fire Chaplain (retired)

Nehemiah was propelled by a passion. He committed himself to rebuild the walls of Jerusalem. As governor of the city, he led by example and with integrity. The explanation of this magnificent man is found in the following phrase:

"because the gracious hand of God was on me."
Nehemiah 2:8 NLT

My academic mentor was Dr. Earle E. Cairns, a brilliant historian of the Christian church. Frequently he prayed for us that the Lord would put His hand on us for good. He prayed the blessing of Nehemiah on us as his students. We have derived immeasurable enrichment over the years as our gracious God answered Professor Cairns' prayer in our lives.

Today may the gracious hand of God be on each reader of this devotion for good. Amen.

Messed Up Companies – Day 66

by Craig Duck – President/Missionary

Read Mark 9:14-24

Encouragement for the day – *"Immediately the father of the child cried out and said, "I believe; help my unbelief!"*

Mark 9:24 ESV

Over the years I have served in some messed up companies. The firefighters assigned to those companies were not perfect. They desired to do a good job; they just didn't work well together. Most of the time they could do nothing right. When I was first promoted to the position of sergeant in the Washington, DC Fire Department, I was transferred to one of those companies. Every time they ran a fire, everything seemed to go wrong for them. It took years of hard work and dedication to change that company around. Together we worked hard at becoming a company that everyone could count on. It just took a lot of focus, drive, and dedication.

In the Christian faith, we are surrounded by imperfect saints. If we honestly examine our lives, we will soon discover that we are just as imperfect. We live in a fallen world, and even though Jesus Christ has changed our life, we still stumble and fall. Check out the heroes of the faith in Hebrews 11. A careful study of the life of those heroes will reveal they struggled with their faith from time to time and even sinned against God. When our faith begins to waver when we find ourselves sliding down the mountain, it's time to look up. The father of the child whom Jesus healed cried out "I believe; help my unbelief!" There are times in our faith journey that we need help. Don't continue to falter; look to God for strength and courage. The same God who made the heroes of the faith what they were will help you to become what you should be.

Lord, give me strength to live a life that is pleasing to you. When I fall, help me to get back up and continue serving you.

Encouragement is the ability to pull someone out of the pit of despair!!

Ready Witness – Day 67

By Wayne Detzler – FCFInternational Board Member and Fire Chaplain

"And Jesus came and said to them, "All authority in heaven and on earth has been given to me. Go therefore and make disciples of all nations, baptizing them in the name of the Father and of the Son and of the Holy Spirit, teaching them to observe all that I have commanded you. And behold, I am with you always, to the end of the age."

Matthew 28:18-20 ESV

When the Holy Spirit awakens the church, it creates a buzz. People start talking about it. In a recent small group at the university, someone asked where we worship. When we mentioned that we are part of Black Rock Church they commented that people are talking about the growth and life we have been experiencing which demands a bigger building. In New Haven people are talking about the fresh life at City Church. It is so easy to witness, when the Holy Spirit is moving. We are simply "giving an answer about the hope that is in us." (1 Peter 3:15 KJV)

Lord teach me how to tell others about your great love. Give me courage today to share it with someone.

Water Supply Officer – Day 68
By Craig Duck – President/Missionary

Read Philippians 4:10-20

Encouragement for the day – *"And my God will meet all your needs according to the riches of his glory in Christ Jesus."*

Philippians 4:19 NIV

An important function on big fires is the water supply officer. In rural areas this assignment can be especially difficult and take many resources to make the operation flow smoothly. Fires need water to be extinguished, and the water supply officer ensures every piece of apparatus that is pumping water on the fire has an adequate supply. Using maps to locate larger water mains, starting drafting operations, or setting up a relay operation are a few of the choices that this officer has at his/her disposal. Running out of water is always dangerous and makes the department look bad. So, the water supply officer ensures all the water needs are met, and the fire extinguished.

We serve a God that can supply all of our needs. There is nothing impossible for Him, and your request for help is not too big. This doesn't mean, however, that everything we ask for will be given to us. Notice how the term "all your needs" is used by Paul. It doesn't say all your wants or desires. Too often we go to God with a "Christmas wish list" of requests. God knows all about us and will gladly give us the things that we are in need of. Paul was thanking the local church in Philippi for supplying his needs when he traveled to Macedonia and Thessalonica. Often God will use His people to help supply the needs that other believers have. We should always be on the lookout for opportunities to help others.

Lord, thank you for this reminder today that you are big enough to supply all the needs I have. May you receive all of the glory.

Encouragement should be a standard operating guideline!!

Pain can provide Purpose – Day 69

By Andrew Starnes – Battalion Chief with a large metro department in NC and FCFInternational Member

Have you ever been in a situation that you worked very hard to achieve only to find out that there is an even bigger mountain to climb? Each personal achievement or success seems to be marked by the challenges of the next step of the journey.

It as if the mountain of adversity shouts at you:

"You didn't think that you were done yet did you?"

If we are not challenged, facing difficult circumstances, or struggles; do we truly grow and learn?

In short, Leadership without opposition, struggles, and challenges is nothing more than a title. To truly understand leadership is to embrace the fact that adversity is a necessary part of our journey. Each day that we face another obstacle we have a choice to make:

Cower and submit or Use it to drive us forward.

Personnel or Boss problems?

Life struggles? Conflicts?

Let's change our disposition by learning from those around us. Analyze as they criticize.

"Seek first to understand rather than to be understood" St. Francis.

As we take one verbal assault after another with a smile because we now realize that they are a test, a mile marker in our journey, and despite their poor disposition we choose to learn from this experience.

Tough times can make us or break us. As a leader, we have chosen to be refined by them and not defined by them.

Each day that we rise to face these trials, let us lift our eyes to the one who has faced it all and remember:

"I can do all things through Christ who strengthens me"
Philippians 4:13 NIV

You are not done yet, and God will "be faithful to complete you" (Philippians 1:6).

Preserving Life – Day 70

By Wayne Detzler – FCFInternational Board Member and Fire Chaplain (retired)

So, it was God! Sometimes it surprises us when we look back and see God's hand at work in our lives. The story of Joseph and his brothers in the Bible explain this. After many years Joseph and his brothers meet. Joseph is a ruler of Egypt, and his brothers are in search of food. The brothers had sold him into slavery, but now they are dependent on him. Joseph puts their minds at ease: *"But don't be upset, and don't be angry with yourselves for selling me to this place. It was God who sent me here ahead of you to preserve your lives. This famine that has ravaged the land for two years will last five more years, and there will be neither plowing nor harvesting. God has sent me ahead of you to keep you and your families alive and to preserve many survivors. So it was God who sent me here, not you! And he is the one who made me an adviser to Pharaoh—the manager of his entire palace and the governor of all Egypt."*

Genesis 45:5-8 NLT

Very often the hardest experiences of our lives have been the portal to the greatest blessing. And this constantly amazes me.

Fire Museums – Day 71

By Craig Duck – President/Missionary

Read Deuteronomy 32:1-7

Encouragement for the day – *"Remember the days of old; consider the years long past. Ask your father, and he will tell you, your elders, and they will teach you."*

Deuteronomy 32:7 HCSB

Yesterday a bunch of us firefighters visited a museum that housed some beautiful fire apparatus. It was amazing to see all the different styles of equipment and think about the people who responded to emergencies on these vehicles. Just ordinary people trying to serve the public like we do today. The attendance was down at the museum we went to. I thought of all the times I visited fire museums over the years and began to think how history might not be important to younger folks. There is a wealth of knowledge and wisdom we can learn from previous generations as we carefully sift through everything housed in a museum.

The Bible encourages us to learn from the past. It is mission critical that one generation pass on to the next Christian values. I love how the Bible records for us all the good, bad, and ugly. It doesn't just sugar coat events and then have us only learn from the good things. Remember, the people of the Bible were just like us. Those who went on to accomplished great things in history had the same fears, questions, and anxieties as we do. They just learned to focus on God rather than what was happening around them. Learning history helps us not to make the same mistakes as previous generations while reminding us of our potential. As we learn from past generations, it should cause us to do great things for God. So, don't just sit on the sidelines as a Christian firefighter or first responder. Read through the Bible, ask older Christians about their faith, and learn what God intends for you to do in the fire service today.

Lord, thank you for this reminder of the importance of history. Help me to faithfully walk in your ways every single day of my life.

Encouragement is the art of pulling people out of the pit of despair!!

Aggressive Interior Firefighters – Day 72

By Keith Helms – International Board Member and retired Battalion Fire Chief with the Charlotte Fire Department

Most fire departments want to be known for their aggressive, interior firefighters. They train and equip their members to safely enter a burning structure to fight the battle at its source. Typically, the Command Staff knows who they can rely on; they also know the firefighters that prefer to stay outside. While I acknowledge that there are times when you have to go defensive, the problem is that there are firefighters who never want to go inside. They refuse to face the challenge of getting close enough to actually engage in the battle. As an IC, I was fortunate to have a battalion (Batt. 4-A) of officers and firefighters that could be counted on to aggressively fight the fire. Going defensive was not the predominate strategy. Getting inside was always the desired approach. Time after time, the crews entered the structure; and time after time, the fire was controlled without further damage to the structure.

We all face a similar problem with sin. Many prefer to deal with sin without dealing with the source. The real problem resides inside. Matthew 23:25- 28 illustrates the difference between an interior attack and an external attack on sin.

"Woe to you, scribes and Pharisees, hypocrites! For you clean the outside of the cup and the plate, but inside they are full of greed and self-indulgence. You blind Pharisee! First clean the inside of the cup and the plate, that the outside also may be clean. Woe to you, scribes and Pharisees, hypocrites! For you are like whitewashed tombs, which outwardly appear beautiful, but within are full of dead people's bones and all uncleanness. So, you also outwardly appear righteous to others, but within you are full of hypocrisy and lawlessness." Failing to be an aggressive, interior "sinfighter" will result in superficial changes. Christ desires followers who will fight sin at its core. He wants changed hearts. His disciples are not afraid to face the interior battle. They are empowered by the Holy Spirit to attack the enemy (Romans 8:12-17), just as good firefighters are trained and equipped for interior firefighting. Face the enemy interiorly; that is where you will find the victory.

Free to Be Like Jesus – Day 73

By John Epps – FCFInternational Member

If you are in Christ, you are free. Not free to sin, but free to serve. Free to live for Him, free to be like JESUS. He is the King. Let's be like The Lord!

The King Is Coming!

"There is therefore now no condemnation to them which are in Christ Jesus, who walk not after the flesh, but after the Spirit. For the law of the Spirit of life in Christ Jesus hath made me free from the law of sin and death."

Romans 8:1-2 KJV

List every way you can think of to be more like Christ the rest of the year:

With My Whole Heart – Day 74

By Wayne Detzler – FCFInternational Board Member and Fire Chaplain (retired)

"I will praise You, O LORD, with my whole heart; I will tell of all Your marvelous works. I will be glad and rejoice in You; I will sing praise to Your name, O Most High."

Psalm 9:1-2 NKJV

King David knew how to worship. He started out singing psalms in the pasture, and he ended up sending psalms to the worship team in Jerusalem. Worship seems to be the very heartthrob of the king. Regularly Ray Bennett and his amazingly gifted family lead our community in worship. These young adults ignite our hearts with praise, worship, and deep thanksgiving. O Lord, help us today to praise you with our whole hearts. Amen.

How can you better worship God today in the fire service?

_____

_____

Incident Action Plan – Day 75

By Craig Duck – President/Missionary

Read Romans 15:1-6

Encouragement for the Day – *"For whatever was written in former days was written for our instruction, that through endurance and through the encouragement of the Scriptures we might have hope."*

Romans 15:4 ESV

Since the introduction of the Incident Command System (ICS) to the fire service, we have learned how to manage incidents. One of the components of ICS is the Incident Action Plan (IAP). The IAP is a way of assisting managers with organizing and planning the incident. The IAP organizes the course of the events within a specific time frame and addresses all phases of the incident in a written document. Within the IAP a detailed list of the various groups and divisions, along with their leaders, is provided to ensure everyone understands the mission. Without an IAP the incident can quickly spiral out of control and firefighters could easily get injured or killed.

Paul reminds the readers of the book of Romans the importance of daily reading and studying the Bible. The Bible is full of helpful principles that Christian firefighters can live by in their departments. When we choose not to follow those principles it leads to chaos and selfishness. Our present-day world exemplifies this truth as we daily watch people injuring and killing one another. The Bible is relevant to today's firefighters, and Paul reminds us that the entire Bible has been written for our instruction. The Bible teaches us how to live in unity, how not to be selfish, how to have patients and how to obtain hope. What is your plan for reading through the Bible? Like an IAP a RTBDP (reading the Bible daily plan) will help us to grow in our knowledge of Biblical principles and become more pleasing to God.

Lord thank you for the Bible which teaches firefighters how to live Godly lives in today's fire service. Help me to read mine every day.

Encouragement – "One beggar showing another beggar where to find bread. " (Martin Luther speaking about evangelism)

Stress – Day 76

By Jonathan Riffe – FCFInternational member

One of the common sources of stress is loss. You can lose your job, your health, your money, your reputation, or a loved one.

When people go through loss, there are always two common reactions. One is fear, and the other is grief. Not once in the Bible does it say, "Grieve not," "Sorrow not," "Weep not," or "Cry not." What it does say is "Fear not." Grief doesn't paralyze, but fear does.

Trust God in the dark valleys, just like David, who prayed in Psalm 23:4, *"Even though I walk through the valley of the shadow of death, I will fear no evil, for you are with me; your rod and your staff, they comfort me."*

"Trust in the Lord with all your heart, and do not lean on your own understanding."
Proverbs 3:5 ESV

"Blessed is the one who trusts in the Lord, who does not look to the proud, to those who turn aside to false gods.
Psalm 40:4 NIV

Keep Growing – Day 77

By Wayne Detzler – FCFInternational Board Member and Fire Chaplain

"My prayer for you is that you will keep growing in spiritual knowledge and insight."
Phil. 1:9 TLB

    As Nero put pressure on the church, Paul focused on love inside the fellowship. My dad had a cruder version: "Either we hang together, or we hang separately." Loving unity in the body of Christ is priority number one. At Black Rock Church we are moving through a transition. As our new church home takes shape, we are meeting in Notre Dame High School. It's a tough time, but our unity is in the Lord. We sing out loud:

"In Christ alone my hope is found;
He is my light, my strength, my song;
This cornerstone, this solid ground,"

Lord, teach me to love those in the body of Christ. May we become united in love, sincerity, and action. May our lives be a sweet-smelling aroma that rises up to you.

Creating Obstacles – Day 78

By Craig Duck – President/Missionary

Read Romans 16:17-27

Encouragement for the day – *"I appeal to you, brothers, to watch out for those who cause divisions and create obstacles contrary to the doctrine that you have been taught; avoid them."*

Romans 16:17 ESV

Like many firefighters and first responders, I love to teach. Over the years I have learned that making obstacles is an excellent way to teach young firefighters. When a recruit comes to an obstacle, he/she must learn how to overcome that barrier and be able to complete the assigned task. Entanglement obstacles, locked doors, and walls that need to be breached are a few of props that we threw together to help students learn. Lately, I have seen other departments that have made bigger and better props. I have seen rapid intervention stations, ladder stations with wires, and propane props that all challenge the student to learn how to overcome obstacles.

Paul cautions us to watch out for people who create obstacles that hinder our walk with Christ. While creating obstacles are good for teaching firefighters' basic principles, it is not good to create them in our faith journey. These obstacles are contrary to what you will learn from Biblical principles and go against everything God has ever taught us. There always seem to be people around us who cause division. They easily stir up strife among believers because of their smooth talk and flattery appeal to earthly emotions. These people don't serve Christ but serve their selfish ambitions. Our obedience to Christ is of more value than a quick worldly passion. Daily reading and studying the Word of God is one way to avoid these obstacles and ensure we are living a life that is pleasing to God.

Lord help me to identify those I meet who are contrary to your will for my life. Help me to stay focused on pleasing you.

Encouraging firefighters and first responders to keep the faith!!

Repent – Day 79

By John Epps – FCFInternational Member

If the scripture stopped with, "For the wages of sin is death", we would have no hope! But Praise God it continues on to say "but the gift of God is eternal life through Jesus Christ our Lord"! Repent and turn to Christ today!

The King Is Coming!

"For the wages of sin is death; but the gift of God is eternal life through Jesus Christ our Lord."

Romans 6:23 KJV

Has there ever been a time when you have surrendered your life to Christ?

What are things that prevent firefighters and first responders from believing in God?

The Need to Vent – Day 80

By Andrew Starnes – Battalion Chief with a large metro department in NC and FCFInternational Member

Have you ever felt the pressures of life, the job, and stress mounting up to such a point that you felt you were going to explode?

As firefighter's we know that pressurized cylinders and containers have devices in place to relieve the pressure if it reaches a dangerous level. These PRV's are there to help alleviate the pressure and bring things back to a manageable level.

What about our own personal need to "alleviate pressure and bring things back to a manageable level?"

What happens when we don't alleviate the pressures of life in healthy ways and we explode on the ones we love? Or, what happens when we don't alleviate the pressures of life and say things we shouldn't to others in person or on social media? Is it fair to our loved ones that "our stressors" have now caused collateral damage to their lives?

Let us consider a new relief valve: A prayer relief valve.

"Let go of anger and leave rage behind! Don't get upset—it will only lead to evil"

Psalms 37:8 CEB

But how do we vent in a healthy way?
Where can we go?
Who can we talk to?

As firefighters, we do everything together, yet we seem to forget that we are not meant to carry these burdens alone.

The Application:

1) There is strength is numbers:

From the very beginning, each of us should seek out a group that we may confide in. They should be a frequent number on our call list.

"Two are better than one because they have a good return for their labor. For if either of them falls, the one will lift up his companion."

Ecclesiastes 4:9 NIV

Let us learn to turn to God and to our group so we can vent in healthy ways instead of blowing up on others.

2) Lift each other up:

"But woe to the one who falls when there is not another to lift him up."

Ecclesiastes 4:9, 10 NASB

Too often we think that we must provide the answers for the troubles that our friends and loved one's face. This is a great failure on our part. Our role is to show up, shut up, and lift up. It is God who ultimately provides the answers and healing. It is our role to be the "hands and feet of Christ" which means to physically show up in the lives of those who are hurting around us.

In closing, we all need someone to vent to. It takes a true friend to let us unload our burdens without thinking we are aiming our frustrations at them. It takes a true friend to tell us what we need to hear and not what we want to hear in those moments.

Let's step up and be that friend to a hurting brother or sister today! You may be the answer to their prayer.

Ultimate Assurance – Day 81

By Wayne Detzler – FCFInternational Board Member and Fire Chaplain (retired)

"If God is for us, who can be against us?" The Apostle Paul presents ultimate assurance. In summary of the treasures of Romans chapter 8, we are reminded that God gave us His Son and with Him we receive everything we ever need. *"If God is on our side, who can ever be against us? Since he did not spare even his own Son for us but gave him up for us all, won't he also surely give us everything else?"* (Romans 8:31-32 Living Bible)

Many years ago, our friend, Sheila Curtis, taught me to sign letters with the phrase, "every blessing." It is snatched directly from this wonderful Bible assurance. May the God of Glory give you every blessing today. Amen.

Why is it so easy for Christian firefighters and first responders to doubt? _____

_____

_____

Being Set Up – Day 82

By Craig Duck – President/Missionary

Read Romans 14:13-17

Encouragement for the day – *"Therefore let us not pass judgment on one another any longer, but rather decide never to put a stumbling block or hindrance in the way of a brother."*

Romans 14:13 ESV

Throughout my career as a firefighter, I have been set up many times. Firefighters and first responders love to play practical jokes, and they take great pleasure in setting another firefighter up. Such was the case when I worked at Engine Company 11 in Washington, DC. There were times when the shenanigans felt like they went on the whole shift. I have been left soaking wet, without a functioning bed, and at the wrong end of laughing firefighters more than once. One time I had misplaced my uniform shirt. For several shifts, I couldn't find it. Finally, one of the firefighters asked for me to make a peanut butter sandwich for him. When I cracked open the jar, there was my shirt stuffed inside.

While practical jokes help to relieve stress in the firehouse, the Bible tells us not to set up a fellow believer for failure. We are told to do everything in love for one another and never to cause a fellow believer to stumble in their faith. In today's text, we learn that some of the early Christians were eating meat that was sacrificed to idols. While many thought the practice was not forbidden by the Bible, others had a problem with the practice. Paul reminded the believers that the "kingdom of God is not a matter of eating and drinking but righteousness and peace and joy in the Holy Spirit" (verse 17). Our mission in life should not be to set people up to stumble in their faith, but rather to encourage them to grow. What have you done to hurt a fellow believer recently? Go to them and ask them for forgiveness and then build them up in the Lord.

Lord, help me today to learn how not to put a stumbling block in front of people. May everything I say and do be pleasing to you.

Encouragement goes a long way when shared with others!!

Loving Justice – Day 83

By Wayne Detzler – FCFInternational Board Member and Fire Chaplain (retired)

"You love justice and hate evil. Therefore God, your God, has anointed you, pouring out the oil of joy on you more than on anyone else."

Psalm 45:7 NLT

The psalmist wrestles with real issues. For instance, he laments the decline of justice in society. He even refers to the collapse of civilization. *"The foundations of law and order have collapsed. What can the righteous do?"* (Psalm 11:3 NLT) Human solutions to this problem all seem to fall short. The media says, it's all going wrong and there's nothing we can do. Politicians protest, my opponents will not allow me to do the right thing. So, our spirits spiral downward into depression and dismay. The psalmist sees it differently. His solution is this. If God is really God, then we can relax in His safe hands. We can actually have joy and gladness, because God is still on the throne!

What is robing you joy today as you serve in the fire service?

___

Fire Shelter – Day 84

By Craig Duck – President/Missionary

Read Psalm 91

Encouragement for the day – *"He who dwells in the shelter of the Most High will abide in the shadow of the Almighty."*

Psalm 91:1

The first recorded use of a fire shelter was in 1804 when a young boy was spared from certain death by a fire in a local prairie. A notation in William Clark's journal mentioned that the boy's mother used a fresh bison hide to cover her son. Since that time fire shelters have dramatically improved. A fire shelter is a last chance piece of equipment that protects firefighters by reflecting radiant heat while trapping breathable air inside the mound-shaped device. The fire shelter is constructed of layers of aluminum foil, woven silica, and fiberglass which can withstand temperatures up to 500 degrees. Firefighters are trained to be able to deploy their fire shelter in the safest location possible in a manner of seconds.

We all go through difficult times in our lives. Whether it's an illness that takes us away from our department, a loss of a friend, divorce, or difficulties with those in our stations, each of us will have times when our lives feel like they are spinning out of control. God desires for every first responder to run to Him for protection and comfort. For those in the fire service who by faith put their trust in the protection of God will find all that they need to weather the storm. Trying to fix our problems on our own is as foolish as not utilizing the fire shelter when needed. God is always ready and willing to help you, are you willing to let Him?

Lord, thank You for carrying me through the difficult times in my life.

Encouraging first responders to keep the faith!!

Pride is Crafty – Day 85

By Jonathan Riffe – FCFInternational member

Pride is crafty. It has a way of bleeding out of us in ways we don't even recognize. Subtly, we project ourselves as the ones who accomplished something when in fact all the credit should go to God.

Our intellect, our natural skills and talents, our health, and our opportunities to succeed all come from God. We have nothing that will enable us to achieve success that we did not receive from God.

"Pride goes before destruction, and haughtiness before a fall."

Proverbs 16:18 NLT

"The pride of your heart has deceived you, you who live in the clefts of the rock, in your lofty dwelling, who say in your heart, "Who will bring me down to the ground?"

Obadiah 1:3 ESV

"If anyone thinks they are something when they are not, they deceive themselves."

Galatian 6:3 NIV

The Jesus Model – Day 86

By Wayne Detzler – FCFInternational Board Member and Fire Chaplain (retired)

Jesus modeled a servant's heart. He constantly taught the priority of serving others. In summary he said:

"For those who exalt themselves will be humbled, and those who humble themselves will be exalted."

Luke 14:11 NLT

This passage of Scripture is a strong contrast. It places humility over against self-exaltation. Many years ago I prayed: "Lord, show me what ministry is all about?" The answer came in one word: serving. I then realized that it was my role to serve the people to whom God called me. Likewise it was my role to serve my children—now also grandchildren and great grandchildren. Finally, it is always my role to serve my dear Margaret. Serving takes different shapes, but it is always our top priority. As Jesus put it; *"For even the Son of Man came not to be served but to serve others and to give his life as a ransom for many."* (Mark 10:45 NLT)

Insanity – Day 87

By Craig Duck – President/Missionary

Read Hebrews 10:19-39

Encouragement for the day – *"And let us keep paying attention to one another, in order to spur each other on to love and good deeds, 25 not neglecting our own congregational meetings, as some have made a practice of doing, but, rather, encouraging each other. And let us do this all the more as you see the Day approaching."*

Hebrews 10:24-25 Complete Jewish Bible

I finished another Insanity workout the other day. As I am approaching 50, it is mission critical for me to work out to continue as a firefighter in a busy company. Workout programs such as Insanity and CrossFit have become popular with the younger firefighters. Recently, I watched some of the CrossFit challenge that Firehouse World in San Diego sponsored at their annual conference. Watching them compete against each other made me want to get back into my routine. One of the reasons why these programs work so well is because you are involved with a network of people who have the same goals as you do. There is something that pushes you to succeed as you come together to exercise. It is far easier for me to quit when I am exercising by myself, so it just makes sense for me to exercise with a group.

    The Bible knows all about working together in a team. The writer of Hebrews encourages us to regularly meet together. When we try to go it alone, we set ourselves up for failure. It is far easier to get discouraged and quit when there is no one else around to cheer you on. Christian firefighters and first responders should understand the importance of regularly attending and participating in a local church. I believe it is also important for Christian first responders to regularly meet together with other Christian first responders for Bible study. Firefighting is very stressful and difficult; fellow believers can help to encourage you in ways most folks don't understand. Get together and study the Bible, try exercising your faith as well as your body.

    Lord, help me to find someone in my department today so we can study the Bible and encourage one another.

Encouragement is good for the soul!!

Make the Call – Day 88

By Andrew Starnes – Battalion Chief with a large metro department in NC and FCFInternational Member

As firefighters, we see pain, tragedy, and death on a regular basis. But then those experiences come to us when:

A close friend dies suddenly...
A family member becomes very sick...
A loved one betrays our trust...
An injury causes a major setback...
A child dies...
A friend commits suicide...

Then with all of the pain around us, those years of trauma erupt to the surface of our souls. We break into pieces and anxiety grips out heart.

What then shall we do?
Our roles become reversed. Those who look to others in their moments of distress are now themselves distressed and in need of rescue.

We Cry out

God, *"Do not be far from me for trouble is near and there is no one to help"*

Psalm 22:11 NIV

Let's not bury our emotions; let them pour out in passionate and overwhelming praise to God. Call upon Him, our families, and the brotherhood. Be honest in these painful moments and realize we are human beings who need help to. This is not a sign of weakness but courage and strength. Remember that God's word tells us: *"For he had not despised or scorned the suffering of the afflicted one; he has not hidden his face from him but has listened to his cry for help"* (Psalm 22:24).

God is waiting on us to cry out. He holds the answers we seek. He holds the comfort we so desperately need. He gives the peace that passes all understanding to those who trust in Him. But we must make the call. As we respond to the call of those who need help in crisis let us remember that God stands ready to respond to the calls of our heart. All we to do is just *"cast our cares upon him for he cares for us."* (1 Peter 5:7).

Call upon God today!

Strength for the Moment – Day 89

By Wayne Detzler – FCFInternational Board Member and Fire Chaplain (retired)

"The LORD gives his people strength. The LORD blesses them with peace."

Psalm 29:11 NLT

Early Yesterday morning I prayed that the Lord would have mercy on us, especially as Margaret was passing through a tough time. Before breakfast time the Elim Park nurse was in our apartment and Margaret and I were on the way to the hospital. At Midstate Hospital in Meriden, CT we met an old friend. Carol came to encourage us through the morning. And a very competent gastroenterologist cleared the deck to help us. This is just one more example of the peace our Lord gives. And we are so thankful to Him. After a night of sleep, I am ready to return to the hospital as we go forward trusting the Lord, who gives us strength.

In what ways this past week has God shown Himself faithful to you? _____

_____

Putting the Pieces Back Together – Day 90
By Craig Duck – President/Missionary

Read Psalm 138

Encouragement for the day – *"Though I am surrounded by troubles, you will protect me from the anger of my enemies. You reach out your hand, and the power of your right hand saves me."*

Psalm 138:7 NLT

    One of the fascinating jobs the fire investigator must do is to put parts of the fire scene back together to find out the cause of the fire. Several times during my stent as the lieutenant of the unit we had to reconstruct equipment, putting all the pieces back together. Once that task was completed, we could then discover what part was responsible for failing, starting the fire. This job can be time consuming when it involves a bomb or a plane. The job, however, can be completed if one remains focused on the tasks at hand.

    There are times in everyone's life when they are let down by someone. Some may even feel that God has let them down in one way or another. But be encouraged today because the last thing God wants is for us is to go through life feeling guilty or carrying shame and regrets.

God is in the business of putting things back together after we have broken them. The Bible is filled with times when ordinary folks like us screwed up and God restored them. Is your life spinning out of control? Stop living your life on your own terms and let God take control. He has the power to not only rescue you out of trouble, but to sustain you in your faith. Begin to daily follow Him wherever He leads you in the fire service, bringing honor and glory to His great name.

Lord, thank you for putting broken lives back together. I stand amazed at what you have accomplished in my life.

Encouraging firefighters and first responders to walk the walk and talk the talk!!

Saving Faith

Congratulations, you have completed the 90-day challenge. We hope and pray that this has been a blessing to you and has helped you to grow in your faith. Perhaps there are some of you firefighters and first responders who have completed the challenge and discovered that you really don't have a relationship with God. Sure, you go through the motions, but something seems to be missing. If you have never had a time in your life when you have asked Jesus Christ to forgive you of your sins and become Lord of your life, I invite you to do so now.

I am not asking you to join a religion, do some kind of work to please God, or complete some ritual. What I am suggesting is that you begin a relationship with God that will radically change your life. The illustration of a fire extinguisher will help you to understand what I am talking about. We all know how to use an ABC fire extinguisher. It is so simple we can easily explain to a child. We also know that the letters stand for common combustibles (wood, paper, cloth, and some plastics), flammable liquids or gases, and energized electrical equipment. When we properly use the fire extinguisher, the fire goes out.

Consider This:

The A in our spiritual extinguisher stands for acknowledge.

A - acknowledge your sins. Romans 3:23, *"For all have sinned and come short of the glory of God."* Romans 6:23, *"For the wages of sin is death, but the gift of God is eternal life in Christ Jesus our Lord."*

The B stands for believe.

B – Believe in God. Acts 16:31, *So they said, Believe on the Lord Jesus Christ, and you will be saved, you and your household."*

C stands for confess.

C – Confess your sins. I John 1:9, *"If we confess our sins, He (Jesus) is faithful and just to forgive us our sins and cleanse us from all unrighteousness."* Romans 10:9, *"that if you confess with your mouth the Lord Jesus and believe in your heart that God has raised Him from the dead, you will be saved."*

So, what are you waiting for? What would stop you from asking God to give you the free gift of eternal life? It is really as simple as that. Right now, wherever you are take a moment and ask God to forgive you of your sins and accept Jesus Christ as your Lord and Savior. You can do this by praying to God.

I promise you, it will be the best decision you will ever make.

If you prayed and asked God to forgive you of your sins, please contact the International Office (FCFImissionary@gmail.com). We have some information we would like to send you to help you with your walk with God in the fire service.

"For by grace you have been saved through faith. And this is not your own doing; it is the gift of God, not a result of works, so that no one may boast."

Ephesians 2:8-9 ESV

Mission Statement – To glorify God in the fire service by building relationships that turn first responders' heart and minds toward Christ (Philippian 2:11), equipping them to serve Him (Ephesians 4:12)

Vision Statement – To encourage one another to share the vision with the fire service through **W**itnessing, **P**raying, **T**eaching the Word, **W**alking worthy.

Contact Information
International Office
249 Rochichi Drive
Boydton, VA 23917
443-336-9859
FCFImissionary@gmail.com

CFHub

www.fellowshipofchristianfirefighters.org

Made in the USA
Columbia, SC
21 September 2019